A Thousand and One

HOUSEHOLD HINTS

A Thousand and One

HOUSEHOLD

HINTS

Editorial Selection by
Gill Davies

BLUE HERON BOOKS

Vancouver

First published in Canada in 2004 by
Blue Heron Books, 9050 Shaughnessy Street
Vancouver, B.C. V6P 6E5
(604) 323-7100
www.raincoast.com

ISBN 1-897035-07-1

Editorial Selection by Gill Davies
Typeset in Great Britain by Antony Gray
Printed and bound in China

Contents

General Disclaimer

While the author and publishers of this volume have acted in good faith as collators of information they can in no way be held responsible or accept liability for any loss or damage arising, howsoever caused.

DISCLAIMER FOR HEALTH SECTION

Always consult or your doctor or therapist if you have high blood pressure or are taking prescription medication.

General Handy Hints

1   Air freshener

Spray aerosol furniture polish behind central heating radiators. The heat will disperse the perfume for some time.

OR . . .

Wipe down radiator with a cloth moistened with a fabric conditioner.

2   Arranging flowers

Never mix cut daffodils in with other cut flowers as they produce a toxin that kills the other blooms.

3 Baking powder

Test baking powder by putting a small amount in hot water. If it bubbles, it is still fresh.

4 Bathroom drawers

Keep these tidy by using plastic containers or trays to hold small items upright.

5 Cavity wall insulation

This greatly reduces the heating costs on an old house and keeps you warmer too.

6   Central heating boilers

Condensing boilers are the most efficient; despite initial high price, they save running costs.

7   Central heating

Turn down the thermostat just a fraction and reduce your annual heating bill.

8   Chimneys

If you have an older house, save money on your heating by blocking up <u>unused</u> chimneys. Plastic foam will do or use old clothing.

9 Clogged drain

If the drain in your sink is clogged, pour ½ cup of baking soda over drain. Then pour a cup of vinegar over it. Leave for a minute until it foams, then pour hot or boiling water down drain. Repeat if necessary.

OR . . .

Use soda crystals.

10 Coffee filter

Turn the stack inside out. It is then easy to extract a single filter.

11 Coffee table

Remove the seat from an old piano stool and tidy up the hinge marks with plastic wood. Fill hollow with collectable (paperweights, small dolls, coins, or souvenirs). Cover with a glass top, cut to fit.

12 Corkboards

Fix a large piece of corkboard on the bedroom wall for your child's (or grandchildren's) drawings and paintings.

AND/OR

Keep one in the kitchen for friends' vacation postcards.

13 Cut flowers

To keep cut flowers fresh for a longer time, mix 2 tablespoons of white vinegar and 2 table-spoons of sugar in a quart of water. Use this in your flower vase.

AND . . .

Before you place the flowers in the vase, cut the base of each stem at an angle.

OR . . .

Add lemonade to water.

14 Dishwashing liquid

This is great for cleaning greasy or soiled hands, after working on the car or in the garden.

15 Dry or water-based paint

This can be disposed of in household garbage collections. Never pour down drains or a storm water sewer.

16 Eco-conscious

Re-use carrier bags and plastic items – they are not biodegradable.

17 Empty containers

Those from very tiny candies, like mints, make good storage holders for needles.

18   Faded carpets

Restore by hand painting with fabric dyes.

19   Flies on windows

To prevent flies landing on a window, rub with cold water and a few drops of paraffin/kerosene.

20   Fluorescent tubes

Old socks can be used to protect the ends of fluorescent tubes in store.

21   Freeze candles

Candles kept in the freezer burn more slowly and evenly.

22 Fresh squeezed lemon juice

Freeze in an ice cube tray. You'll have small amounts for recipes that need 1 or 2 tablespoons. Thaw in microwave or drop into hot sauces.

OR . . .

Drop a cube into a glass of ice water to freshen it up.

23 Fridge/Freezer

Ensure that food has cooled before putting in the fridge or freezer, otherwise your fridge works overtime to cool the food.

24 Fridges & freezers

To run efficiently:
Don't place the appliance too close to your oven
DO . . .
Defrost regularly
AND . . .
Try to keep at least ¾ full.

25 Frosting windows

A temporary frosting for privacy can be made
with 1 tablespoon of Epsom Salt to 1 cup of
beer. Brush on window and leave to dry. It can
be washed away again with ammonia.

26 Furniture restoration

To make furniture look older, paint with varnish mixed with soot.

27 Garage ideas

Simplify reversing by hanging an old tennis ball from the ceiling so that it just touches the centre of the rear car window when it is parked properly.

28 Hammering water pipes

Turn down your water pressure at the stopcock.
OR . . .
Buy a 'waterhammer' at the hardware store which can be easily installed in the line.

29 Heat marks on polished furniture

Make up a paste with cigarette ash and olive oil. Apply to the mark and then rub off.

OR . . .

Pour a little linseed oil on mark and then sprinkle with sugar. Wipe off once the sugar is absorbed.

30 Heat stains on stainless steel

Hot stainless steel surfaces on toasters or kettles stain easily if they come in contact with plastic bags. Remove with nail varnish remover.

31 Hiccups

Drink water from the back of a glass.

OR . . .

Suck an ice cube or slice of lemon.

OR . . .

Apply an ice cube to the side of the neck.

32 House plants

If you have an aquarium, save the water each time you change it to water your house plants. They will thrive on this.

33 Ice cubes

When filling ice cube box in the freezer, add a few mint leaves, thin slices of lime or lemon, or even rose petals – to add extra flavour.

34 Insulate to conserve heat

Insulate your loft to save a lot of lost and wasted heat.

35 Insulation

Insulate your loft with just 6" thickness can save you quite a lot per annum.

Cavity-wall insulation can reduce the heating bill and keep you warmer too. For safety, make sure that your ventilation grilles are not blocked, especially if you are using gas or solid fuel.

36 Ketchup, mayonnaise or syrup

Keep these in pump bottles. They are easier to control than glass or squeezy bottles, especially for young children.

37 Kitchen smells

Fill a lidless jar with a some vanilla pods.

38 Labels

Use masking tape to label foods or spices with the date of purchase.

39 Lemon grass

Frozen lemon grass tea can be made into ice cubes that will give extra zip when added to cold water.

40 Life span (average) of domestic appliances

Central air conditioner – 15 years
Clothes dryer – 18 years
Dishwasher – 12 years
Freezer (upright) – 20 years
Kitchen stove – 18 years
Refrigerator – 17 years
Room air conditioner – 12 years
Washing machine – 13 years
Water heater – 13 years

41 Masking tape

Use masking tape to seal food bags and other packages.

42 Meatballs

Mix ingredients in a bowl. On a cutting board, flatten mixture into a rectangle. Cut lengthwise and then horizontally with a sharp knife to make squares.

ALSO . . .

Before rolling into balls, wet your hands or coat them with flour to stop mix sticking to you.

43 Mildew

Brush on household bleach, then wipe away (test a small area first).
OR . . .
Wipe with lemon juice.

44 Old telephone directory

Keep an old telephone book in the car as a useful reference
OR . . .
Swap with someone from another area so you have a wider range of information.

45 Packing crockery

If moving house, pack crockery while it is still wet. Breakages are less likely.

46   Paint disposal

If you have more paint than you need . . .
Apply another coat.
AND THEN . . .
Keep some for touching up any later scratches
or marks.
AND THEN . . .
Give any excess to your local drama group for
set painting.

47   Painting steps

Paint every other step, let dry, then paint the
alternate steps. You can maintain access via the
dry steps.

48 Patching up wallpaper

Always use a piece that you have torn by hand – not cut – and tear toward the wrong side of the wallpaper. Then the patch will be practically invisible.

49 Peeling onions

Burn a candle close by when cutting or chopping onions. This stops the tears flowing!

50 Picnic tablecloth

Use an old single fitted sheet. It stays secure and is easy to wash.

51 Pillows

To restore fluffiness in pillows, put them in the clothes dryer.

52 Plastic containers

Stop tomato based stains by rubbing the inside with vegetable oil before placing food in container.

53 Plastic containers

Use these for storing items in the fridge.
OR . . .
For storing threads and other haberdashery.
OR . . .
Pierce bases with a hot soldering iron and use as
seed trays.

54 Rear car lights

Hang an old mirror on the rear wall of the garage
so that the car lights can be checked before you
leave home.

55 Recycling

Look for the recycle symbol on plastic bottles, cartons and bags and help reduce unnecessary waste.

ALSO . . .

Use your local council's recycling to have your 'garbage' collected from your home.

OR . . .

Take papers, bottles, cans, etc to the recycling banks, often in supermarket car parks.

56 Recycling

Try to buy products in packaging that has been recycled and is recyclable and bio-degradable. Look for the recycle symbol.

57 Reheating food economically

It is cheaper and quicker to reheat food in the microwave.

OR . . .

A slow cooker.

OR . . .

A pressure cooker.

58 Remember the three R's

Reduce, recycle and repair.

59 Repairing burned carpet

Cut away any singed or melted areas. Find a discreet spot, hidden or close to the wall, and clip a section of carpet. Glue it over burned spot.

60 Re-use carrier bags

Recycle clean spare bags and use these again.

61 Running list

Keep list on your fridge or notice board of small jobs that need to be done around the house or garden for those spare moments you and the rest of the family suddenly discover.

62 Save fridge and freezer running costs

Ensure that food is cool before putting in the fridge or freezer.

63 Save waste

Use refill pouches and cartons for detergents.

64 Sewing tough material or carpet

Rub the fabric first with an old candle or cooking paraffin/kerosene.

65 Squeaking door hinges

Let a few drops of oil run down through the hinge as you move it to and fro. Have a paper towel ready to catch any drips. Wipe away excess.

66 Squeaky floorboards

These can be improved by using French chalk or talcum powder.

67 Sticky desk drawer

Rub a candle on the runners of the drawer.

68 Sticky labels

WD40 will remove sticky labels. Just spray a little on the label and leave for a few minutes. Then label simply slides off.

69 Sticky labels on glass

Smooth straight (not chunky) peanut butter on labels on glass, bottles, or mirrors. More than one application may be needed.

70 Stop glass cracking

A teaspoon in a glass will take the heat and prevent a glass cracking when very hot water is poured into it.

71 Stuck zipper

Draw on the teeth of the zipper with a pencil.
OR . . .
Put a little lip balm on the teeth. Work zipper up and down until it moves smoothly.

72 Suede shoes

Sticking tape or masking tape will remove dust and dirt without damaging shoes.

73 Take refuse to be recycled

Take newspapers, clothing and bottles to the recycling banks.

74 Temperature at home

Aim to keep a room warm and comfortable at about 70°F or 21°C.

75 Tight electric plugs

If an electric plug fits too tightly and is difficult to remove, rub its prongs with a soft lead pencil.

76 Toilet leak test

Add food colouring to the toilet tank. Do not flush for 30 minutes. If the water in the toilet bowl changes colour, your tank is leaking.

77 Toy bag

Hang a vinyl shoe bag on the back of the bedroom door for small toys, teddies, dolls, pens and so on.

78 Turning a screw

To remember which way to turn a screw, say, 'Lefty Lucy, Righty Tighty'.

79 Use a pump bottle for dish liquid

These fit in smaller spaces and can be kept out handy.

80 Useful tools

Keep the following handy:

Oil can, pliers, screw drivers (regular and Phillips head), a hammer, nails, tacks and picture hangers.

81 Wallpaper and painting

If using a bucket of paste or paint, tie a taut piece of string over the top between the handles. Excess paint or paste can be wiped off, to drop back into bucket. The brush can then rest on the string, its handle on the rim, and any drips will go into the bucket.

82 Wallpaper pasteboard

Clean off excess paste with a plastic scraper before wiping down with a cloth to reduce build-up on cloth.

OR . . .

Cover board with a plastic sheet or disposable plastic tablecloth which can be thrown away afterwards.

83 Washing laundry

Use a lower wash temperature or economy wash (to use existing hot water)
AND . . .
Do not underfill – always wash full loads.

84 Watering Plants

Use the water from boiling eggs, cooled, to water plants.

85 Water heating costs

Having a shower rather than a bath uses far less water and cuts costs considerably.

ALSO . . .

Save money by not leaving taps/faucets dripping.

ALSO . . .

Insulate your tank with a jacket.

86 Water marks on mahogany

Make up a paste with coffee granules and a little warm water. Leave paste on mark overnight and then polish off.

87 Watering houseplants

Use rainwater, rather than tap water to water plants.

AND . . .

In winter, use melted snow: it contains minerals that are good for plants.

88 Weekend list

On Sunday evening put a list on the fridge or notice board of jobs to be done NEXT weekend (tidy drawers, defrost fridge, sow seeds etc.). Add to this through the week. Crossing the items off later gives a fine sense of achievement!

89 When you run out of mothballs . . .

Put leftover soap slivers in a vented plastic bag. The scent will keep moths away and the clothes smell good.

Cleaning

1   Acrylic baths

Never use harsh abrasives. Rub with washing-up liquid or liquid soap. Rub stubborn stains with fine sandpaper until smooth, then use silver metal polish and rinse well.

2   Adhesive removal

Scrape off as much of the paper from label as possible.

THEN . . .

Apply thinner followed by rubber cement (from art or office suppliers). Rub with a cloth or paper towel. This works well on glass, Formica and non-porous surfaces but will cloud some plastics. Take care as rubber cement is very flammable.

OR . . .

Lighter fluid often will remove rubber-based adhesives.

OR . . .

Use vinegar to remove adhesive from glass jars or the sink.

OR . . .

Use white spirit.

OR . . .

Fingernail polish remover.

OR . . .

Avon 'Skin-so-Soft' will remove sticky residue left from labels or tape (or grease)– from glasses, windows, walls and plastic dishes. Wash with soapy water afterwards.

OR . . .

Use methylated spirits/denatured alcohol. This

will work for residue left by sticking tape, decals, stickers, sticking plaster and price stickers – on wood, glass, metal and plastic. It can be used on skin, too. It is flammable so take care.

3   Bad oven odours

Strong smells left by oven cleaners disappear if you bake orange peel in the oven for a few minutes.

4   Baking soda

This is non abrasive and cleans many household items – a good all-round cleaner

5   Bamboo furniture

Scrub bamboo or cane furniture with borax in warm soapy water. Wash unpainted wicker and bamboo with salt water to stiffen and bleach it.

6   Bathroom mirrors

Rub with a cloth dipped in glycerine (or glycerine and methylated spirits/denatured alcohol) to reduce fogging.

7   Bathroom odours

A shallow dish of baking soda behind toilet absorbs bathroom odours.

OR . . .

Light a match over the toilet bowl to disperse methane gas odours.

8   Black furniture

Cracks and chips on black furniture and ceramics can be painted with black nail polish.

9   Brass cleaning

Boil small brass objects in water with salt and vinegar. Wipe dry and polish with brass cleaner.

10   Bread containers

Add a drop of vinegar to the water when cleaning a bread-bin, to deter mould.

11   Brooms and mops

A strip of foam or sponge around tops of broom and mop handles prevents marks on walls – and stops their slipping to the floor.

12   Burned pans

Put ½ cup of baking soda in pan and ½ fill with water. Boil until burnt particles float to top.

13   Burnt plastic

If plastic burns on a toaster, rub with eucalyptus oil.

14 Carpet cleaning

If furniture must be replaced before your carpet is completely dry after shampooing, put drink coasters under legs to prevent stains or dents.

15 Cat litter smells

To keep litter smelling fresh, mix baby powder in with it.

16 Ceramic bathroom tile walls

Use furniture polish to clean ceramic tile walls (not floors). It stops a soap film building up. Smooth, rub with silver metal polish and rinse.

17 Chandeliers

Use a squirt of washing-up liquid and $\frac{1}{4}$ cup of ammonia in a bucket of warm water.

18 Chenille bedspreads

Wash these on a breezy day. Hang inside out and the chenille on one side fluffs up the pile on the other.

19 Chrome

Brighten chrome by rubbing with plain flour.
Or . . .
Use ammonia on a cloth. Wash off and polish with a clean cloth.

20 Cleaning a bathroom

Run shower at hottest setting and close door until everywhere is steamy. Then wipe with a cloth.

21 Cleaning a candlestick

Place it in deep freezer for one hour. Then wax will chip off much more easily – especially good for glass candlesticks.

22 Cleaning a coffee grinder

Grind up a cup or so of rice in the grinder to clean it and sharpen its blades.

23 Cleaning a toilet or any vitreous china

Drop in two indigestion tablets, wait twenty minutes, brush, and flush.

24 Cleaning a vase

To remove a stain from the bottom of a glass vase or cruet, fill with water and drop in two indigestion tablets.

25 Cleaning aluminium

Aluminium window and door frames will shine if you rub them with a cloth dipped in ammonia.

26 Cleaning barbecue grid

Screw up a ball of foil and rub the grilling grid until clean.

27 Cleaning bathroom tiles

Sprinkle a little boric acid on tiles before washing.

28 Cleaning brass handles

Put cardboard collars around brass fittings to protect timber.

29 Cleaning casserole dishes

If food is stuck, fill dishes with boiling water and add 3 tablespoons of baking soda or salt. Leave for an hour.

30 Cleaning clear glass shower doors

Spray with carpet/fabric spot remover. Sponge over and rinse.

31 Cleaning cushion covers

Make sure you replace piped loose cushion covers while still slightly damp; otherwise the piping can shrink and tighten.

32 Cleaning disposal units

Freshen a garbage disposal unit by sprinkling with baking soda and a few drops of dishwashing fluid. With a new toilet brush, scrub under the rubber gasket and around the inside. Then turn on water and the disposal and flush thoroughly.

33 Cleaning fridges

Make sure power is off. Then wipe refrigerators and freezers with warm water and soap. Wipe down with vanilla essence or leave an open packet of bicarbonate of soda inside to absorb odours.

34   Cleaning grout in tiled surfaces

A quick method of doing this is to use a mixture of lemon juice and hot water. Approximately 50% mixture. Simply scrub the mixture into the grouting using a toothbrush and rub off using a clean cloth.

35   Cleaning hands

After working on the car, clean hands with a mixture of dishwashing liquid and sugar.
AND . . .
Use olive oil or cooking oil to clean hands dirtied by engine oil.

36 Cleaning high windows

Use a spray bottle attachment that fits a garden hose.

37 Cleaning lampshades

Use an old shaving brush to clean pleated or ruffled shades.

38 Cleaning mirrors

Air-freshener works well and smells good.

39 Cleaning paint rollers

Hold roller frame vertically and place it on a paint tray. Slip loop of wire paint roller cleaner over top of paint roller. Hold firmly and slide cleaner.

40 Cleaning pine

Hot water can turn pine yellow. Use cold water and soap to remove grease and dirt.

41 Cleaning shower doors

Wipe with lemon oil to remove any build-up and keep doors protected a little longer.

42 Cleaning under a refrigerator

Sweep a stick underneath fridge to remove loose dirt. Finish cleaning with a piece of cloth, soaked in a floor-cleaning product and tied around stick.

43 Cleaning woodwork

Try using cold tea.

44 Clearing the table

Pile everything into a large dishpan so only one journey is needed.

45　Cloudy drinking glasses

Soak glasses for at least an hour in slightly warm white vinegar (not boiled). Use a nylon net or plastic scrunchie to remove film. This will not work if the damage is tiny scratches after dishwashing.

46　Condensation on mirrors

Wipe down mirrors with a damp cloth and washing up liquid and let dry naturally. The mirror will stay clear for about 6 weeks.

47 Condensation on windows

Use half a potato and rub across the surface of the window. Then buff.

48 Cork floors

These can be mopped if sealed, but do not over-wet or the cork may crack. Add two tablespoons of methylated spirits/denatured alcohol to a bucket of water.

49 Crayon on walls or washable wallpaper

Spray with multipurpose lubricating oil. Gently wipe with a paper towel. If stubborn, sprinkle baking soda on a damp sponge and rub in circles. Dip a sponge into dilute dishwashing fluid in water and rub away remaining lubricant. Rinse with a sponge of plain water. Dry with a clean cloth.

OR . . .

Use a blow dryer to heat the wax, which should then wipe away. If any staining remains, wet a cloth with bleach and wipe.

50 Dark leather furniture

Clean once a year with castor oil to prevent cracking.

51 Deodorising plates and containers

Remove pungent smells from dishes, utensils, pans, and cutting boards by adding ¼ cup of lemon juice to dishwater.

52 Dishwasher

Run vinegar through the dishwasher once a month to deter hard deposits.

53 Drawer liners

Cut several thicknesses of paper for each drawer. When they need relining, a clean paper lining will be waiting below the old one.

54 Dull laminated worktops

Polish with a cut-and-polish car cleaner to restore shine.

55 Electric blankets

Store between the mattress and base to keep clean and flat.

56 Electrical cords

Clean dirty marks off electrical cords with a clean cloth and a few drops of eucalyptus oil.

57 Fabric lampshades

These can be vacuumed lightly.

58 Fingerprints

Spray starch doors and painted walls in hallways and stairways. The coating resists grease and fingerprints.

59 Fireplace smells

After you clean out the ashes, reduce smells by placing a shallow pan of baking soda in the fireplace for a few hours.

60 Fish smells

Obliterate fish odours – or any unpleasant food smells – by putting a bowl of white vinegar in the area for a few hours.

61 Foggy windscreen

Rub with an eraser from the stationery store.

62 Freezer cleaning

After defrosting, wipe freezer with a little glycerine. Ice will peel away easily next time you defrost.

63 Freshening bedding

If bedding such as pillows or wool underlays is difficult to wash, put it in a strong plastic bag. Insert vacuum cleaner nozzle in tightly gripped neck of bag to remove dust and mites.

64 Freshening up white grout

Cover grout with white liquid shoe polish. Wipe away any spills on surrounding tiles.

65 Furniture marks on carpet.

To remove the indentation marks left by heavy furniture on carpets place ice cubes on top of the indentation area. When half the ice cubes have melted, remove the remaining ice then using a stiff brush simply fluff up the carpet pile so that it looks normal and leave to dry naturally. For short pile carpets a stiff nylon fingernail brush is ideal.

66 Furniture polish

Make your own: Shake and mix together one-third of a cup each of turpentine, boiled linseed oil and vinegar. Buy pre-boiled linseed oil at a hardware store or paint shop.

67 Garlic, onion or fish smells on hands

Rub hands over a stainless steel utensil under running water.

68 Gas stove hot plates

Remove burners and clear any clogged holes with fine wire. Soak in detergent, scrub with a plastic scourer, then rinse and shake out water. Wipe stove top and replace burners.

69 Glass oven doors

Clean glass doors on wood burners or ovens with paper towels soaked in brown vinegar. Spread paper on glass, leave for about 15 minutes, and then wipe clean.

70 Glass shower doors

Clean with white vinegar on a sponge.

71 Glass tabletops

Rub tops with lemon juice. When dry, polish with crumpled newspaper.

72 Grease or food on worktops or stove

Sprinkle baking soda on grease splatters or dried food and then rub with a wet sponge. Rinse with clean sponge. Repeat if needed.

73 Grease stains on the carpet

Shake with corn starch and leave for at least 8 hours. Then vacuum.

74 Grease stains on wallpaper

Mixing corn starch and water into a paste. Rub on with a soft, clean cloth. Test a small area first.

75 Holland blinds

Try using a soft eraser to remove stains.

76 Ink stain removal (clothes)

Rub alcohol on the stain and then wash.

77 Ink stain removal (walls)

Wipe with bleach.

78 Insects on the car

Baking soda will clean away bugs and is non abrasive.

79 Keeping a chimney clean

Throw a handful of salt on the fire.

80 Keeping the shower clean

Hang a squeegee in the shower and ask the family to quickly wipe down walls after use so soap scum does not accumulate.

81 Kitchen sponges

If regular cellulose kitchen sponges get smelly, give them quick spray of Fabreeze (or any fabric odour remover).

OR . . .

Put through the dishwasher cycle.

82 Leather furniture

Clean with saddle soap. Use very little water. Allow to dry, buff with a soft cloth.

83 Loo rings

Flush so bowl sides wet, then apply a paste of borax and lemon juice. Leave for two hours before scrubbing.

84 Lunch box or plastic container smells

Soak a piece of white bread in white vinegar and leave in the closed lunch box overnight.

OR . . .

Freeze empty containers.

OR . . .

Leave containers in the sun for several hours.

OR . . .

Place a piece of lemon in container and replace lid. Leave for a few days.

85 Making a cheap cleaning agent

Mix 1 part bleach to 10 parts water in a spray bottle. Do label bottle clearly.

86 Making a disposal unit smell fresh

Throw in some chopped lemons or limes and run them through. Use plenty of water.

87 Marks inside cups and mugs

These sometimes occur when metal cutlery damages the glaze coating and can be improved with whitening toothpaste.

88 Mattress

Mattresses can be vacuumed or briskly brushed with a broom. Surface wash with almost-dry detergent suds and air thoroughly.

89 Metal shower head

If clogged, remove and boil in half a cup of vinegar and two litres of water for 15 minutes.

90 Microwave odours

In between using microwave, keep a cup of baking soda in there.

91 Microwave spills

To clean baked-on food, fill a measuring cup full of water and turn the microwave on for about 1–2 minutes, until the water boils. Then all the old food wipes off easily.

92 Mirror cleaning

After cleaning, rub glass mirrors vigorously with dry newspaper. The ink and sizing helps make a good finish.

93 Moth deterrent

Blocks of camphor prevent mustiness and deter moths and silverfish.

94 Moving heavy items

Wear rubber gloves when moving refrigerators or washing machines. You'll have a firmer grip.

95   Musty instrument cases

Use Damp Rid to remove must. Shut the Damp Rid in the case and leave it undisturbed, without moving or opening the case, for several weeks.

96   Nail polish remover

This will remove old wall paper glue, melted plastic, paint spatters from windows and tub insert.

97   Net curtain cleaning

Hang the curtains with white Velcro strip fastened on to the window frame. Then they can be quickly removed and replaced.

98 Noisy bedsprings

Spray lubricant on bedsprings to stop them squeaking.

99 Old decals

These can be carefully removed from glass with a razor blade.

100 Paint on carpet

Spray with window cleaner and wipe clean.

101 Pale leather furniture

Use petroleum jelly on pale leather. Wipe excess off with a soft cloth.

102 Paper and parchment lampshades

Turn off power. Clean with a feather duster and rub away spots with a piece of dry bread. Wipe light bulbs with a damp cloth.

103 Permanent marker on carpet

Soak a washcloth or flannel in rubbing alcohol and then dab on stain. Do not rub – just keep blotting and turning cloth to a clean part.

104   Pet accidents: urine on carpet

Blot with paper towels. Mix one teaspoon of mild dish-washing detergent in a cup of warm water, Dip a clean towel in liquid and dab stain. Do not over-wet. Rinse with fresh water and blot dry. Mix $1/3$ cup white vinegar with $2/3$ cup water and dab on stain. Rinse and then blot dry. 24 hours on, sprinkle carpet with baking soda or rug deodoriser. Vacuum a few hours later.

105 Plastic container stains

Rub baking soda paste (baking soda and water) into any stains. Rinse with vinegar and wash normally.

OR . . .

Put container outside in sunshine and stains will be bleached away.

106 Plastic shower heads

Soak in equal amounts of hot vinegar and water. Do not boil.

107 Plastic showers

Clean moulded fibre cabinets with a mixture of equal parts of brown vinegar and kerosene.

108 Polishing chrome

Rub with a crumpled up piece of aluminium foil.

109 Polishing copper

Rub with ketchup. Leave for five minutes. Then rinse off with hot water and dry to a shine.

110 Polishing jewellery

Drop 2 indigestion tablets into a glass of water and immerse jewellery for 2 minutes.

111 Polishing silver

Put damp baking soda on a soft cloth and polish to a shine.

112 Polishing

Never apply spray polish to furniture directly; put it on a duster and rub on. Then polish. This prevents build-up of excess polish, which is wasteful and difficult to remove.

113 Porcelain

If a porcelain bath has yellowed, rub with a solution of salt and turpentine.

114 Preventing grimy residue on refrigerator top

After cleaning, lay old cloth placemats there.

115 Preventing stains in plastic containers

Spray container with cooking spray before using.

116 Refrigerators

Baking soda will clean the outside of a refrigerator.

AND . . .

It restores whiteness to yellowed fridges.

117 Removing burn marks off a saucepan

Boil rhubarb in it.

118 Removing candle wax from carpet or fabric

Scrape away excess. Place an iron on top of a cloth over the wax and it will stick to the cloth instead of the carpet. If a stain remains, leave a sprinkling of baking soda overnight and then vacuum.

119 Removing chewing gum

Place ice in plastic bag and hold on fabric or carpet for three minutes. Blot with lemon juice. Wipe. Repeat if needed.

120 Removing crayon

Rub lightly with a dry, soap-filled steel wool pad

OR . . .

Use a damp cloth sprinkled with baking soda.

121 Removing mildew off a shower curtain/drape

Rub with baking soda or a mild bleach solution, then rinse in clean water.

122 Removing red wine stains from a carpet

Pour on cold water or soda water and then pat dry.

123 Removing scuff marks from vinyl luggage

Rub lemon extract over area.

124 Removing sticky labels from plastic

If label has been wet, or the item has been stored somewhere hot or humid, it may be more difficult to remove.

Test in an inconspicuous area to check remover will not damage surface. Then dampen a piece of cloth or a cotton bud with dry cleaning fluid. Leave fluid just long enough to allow the label to be rubbed off. Then wipe away excess quickly and wash item in soapy water.

125 Rocking chair marks

Protect shiny floors by gluing felt weather stripping under rockers.

126 Rubbing away scratches

Rub small scratches on china with toothpaste.

127 Rust

Rust on metal furniture can be scrubbed off with turpentine.

128 Save extra trips

Gather dusters, polish, cleaning agents and so on into a plastic bucket. Take this with you as you clean.

129 Sawdust clean-up

Sawdust can clean away grease or paint from hands. Wet your hands and rub with sawdust. It's safer and cheaper than a solvent or commercial cleaners.

130 Scratches on furniture

Light scratches can be disguised with a wax crayon pencil.

OR . . .

Rub with a Brazil-nut.

131 Scuff marks

Marks caused by shoes on vinyl floors can be removed by wiping with eucalyptus oil on a cloth.

132 Scuff marks on walls

Remove scuff marks or pen, and pencil stains with a dry cloth and rubbing alcohol.

133 Separating stuck photos

Use a hair dryer on a low setting and gently melt them apart.

134 Slimy sponges

Rinse loofahs and natural sponges under cold tap and then soak for an hour in two tablespoons of vinegar to one litre of water.

135   Small dents in furniture

These can be steamed with a steam iron over a dampened cloth. Try not to overheat delicate items and be hyper-cautious with valuable pieces.

136   Smelly sports sneakers

Fill knee-high stockings with unused pet litter and baby powder. Tie ends and leave in shoes overnight.

OR . . .

Put a few teaspoons of baking soda in centre of a cotton cloth. Tie cloth and use a rubber band to secure edges. Leave in shoes overnight. These will work in any kind of shoe and can be reused.

137 Stained bathroom tiles

Make a paste of bicarbonate of soda and bleach. Scrub and rinse.

138 Stains on a porcelain enamel bath

Make a paste of cream of tartar, diluted hydrogen peroxide and a few drops of ammonia. Leave mixture on bath for two hours before washing away.

139 Stains on ceramics

Rub coffee, tea or cigarette burns on china and ceramics with a damp cloth dipped in baking soda.

140 Sweetening a linen closet or airing cupboard

Spray cotton balls with your favourite scent. Once they are dry place them in the corners and on the shelves.

141 Tarnished silverware

Line a cake pan with aluminium foil. Fill with 1 tablespoon of baking soda per 2 cups of water and heat in oven to C150°. Lay silverware in pan, touching aluminium foil. Stains disappear.

142 Thermos flasks

To refreshen, fill the bottle with water, drop in four indigestion tablets, and leave to soak for an hour (or longer).

143 To freshen a sour sponge

Soak sponge in lemon juice and rinse out. This will remove the odour but you still need to microwave or dishwash your sponge to prevent bacteria growing.

144 To make a saucepan shine

Boil rhubarb in saucepan.

145 To remove rust from chrome

Wipe it with aluminium foil dipped in Coke.

146 To remove stickers

Saturate decals, glue or stickers with vegetable oil and they should then rub off furniture, glass or plastic.

147 Unclogging a drain

Drop three indigestion tablets down a sink drain, followed by a cup of white vinegar. Wait a few minutes, then run hot water though.

148 Vacuuming small gaps

If a vacuum nozzle is too big to fit into small dust traps, attach inner cardboard roll from plastic wrapping or foil to vacuum cleaner hose, flatten the end to fit into the gap and suck away dust.

149 Venetian blinds

Wear an old pair of fabric gloves. Dip fingers in warm soapy water and run each slat between fingers.

150 Vitreous glass

Use paper towels soaked in brown vinegar. Spread paper on glass, leave for 15 minutes, and then wipe clean.

151 White heat marks and water rings on furniture

Provided wood has a good finish, remove marks with equal parts of baking soda and white, non-gel toothpaste. Lightly dampen a soft, white cloth and dip into the paste. Gently rub. Then wipe clean, and buff to a shine. Follow with furniture polish.

OR . . .

Dip a cloth in vegetable oil, then in cigarette ash. Rub the mark.

OR . . .

Rub mayonnaise onto stain, leave overnight, then wipe with a dry towel.

152 Washing windows

Do this on a dull day: they dry too fast and streak in sunshine.

153 White paintwork

White correction fluid can touch up chips in paintwork and vacuum cleaner marks on skirting boards.

154 Window cleaning advice

Clean inside of window vertically – and outside, horizontally. Then you can detect which side a smear is on.

155 Window cleaning finish

After cleaning, rub vigorously with dry newspaper. The ink and sizing helps make a good finish.

156 Windows

Warm water and add ammonia to it. Rinse and wipe over.

157 Wine stains on clothes

Stretch stained area over a bowl, sprinkle with salt, and then pour boiling water over. If fabric or bowl cannot take boiling water, use as hot as possible.

158 Wine stains: recent

For fresh wine stains while still wet, soak with soda water and dry with a clean dry cloth.

159 Wooden floorboards

Add a capful of linseed oil to water for shine and scent. Use as little water as possible.

160 Worktops

Soak a cloth in bicarbonate of soda and leave it on top of dried-on spots for half-an-hour. Then wipe off.

Laundry

1   Avoid fading

Turn dark clothes inside out and wash in coolest water possible; dry at lowest heat.

2   Ball point ink stains

Rub with a cotton bud soaked in eau-de-cologne.

3   Beer stains on wool

Salt fixes some stains but works on beer – scrub with lukewarm water and salt.

4   Bleeding colours

If colours run onto other garments, do not dry spoiled articles. Wash again IMMEDIATELY with regular detergent and colour-safe bleach.

5   Blood stains

Pour peroxide on blood and rinse with cold water. Repeat if needed.

6   Burn marks on iron

Rub with aluminium foil.

7   Burn or scorch marks on washable items

Brush gently or use dry sponge to remove loose particles. Wash with regular detergent and colour-safe bleach.

8   Chewing gum on clothing

Place ice in a plastic bag and hold onto gum for 3 minutes. Blot with lemon juice and wipe.

9   Deodorant stains on garments

Soak stain with white vinegar for 30 minutes. Launder in the hottest water safe for the fabric. Use an enzyme detergent or a detergent with bleach after checking care labels.
OR . . .
Cover stain with liquid detergent, leave for 5 to 10 minutes, then wash.

10 Fabric softening

Pour 2 capfuls of fabric conditioner onto a clean dish towel. Place in dryer with garments. To reduce static, use fresh softener every 15 loads or so.

11 Fabric

For softening, swish a washcloth in a mixture of fabric softener and water, squeeze out and place in dryer.

12 Petrol on clothing

Use another oil-based product to draw out odour. Baby oil works well. Put some into washer with garment. Leave for a while before adding detergent.

13 General stains on washable clothing

Try cleaning fluid, spot remover, or petroleum-based pre-wash spray. Place garment stain-side down on paper towels and dab with cleaner on a towel or brush. Move paper towels to keep a clean area under stain to absorb it. If stain persists, treat with pre-wash spray and launder.

14 Gum on clothing

Brush egg white onto gum with a toothbrush. Leave for 15 minutes and then launder normally.

15 Ink stains

Rub alcohol on stain before washing.

16 Laundering quilted or down jackets

Check there are no weak seams. Spot-clean stains or grime on cuffs and then wash gently. Rinse well. Tumble-dry until lining fluffs up (knotted towels or tennis balls in dryer help this). Air outdoors.

17 Laundry basket

Every week place a fabric softener sheet in the bottom of laundry basket

OR . . .

Sprinkle baking soda in the bottom of basket to absorb odours.

18 Lint prevention

Never wash dark clothes with towels or washcloths.

19 Lipstick removal

Use petroleum jelly to remove stains
OR . . .
Rub in a little vegetable shortening and then wash as normal.

20 Mildew

Shake or brush to remove loose particles. Pre-soak in cold water. Wash in hot water with strong detergent. Bleach can be added to whites. Or use colour-safe bleach. Dry well: heat and sun kill mildew.

21 Net or lace curtains/drapes

Re-hang after laundering, arrange folds, then spray lightly with fabric finish.

22 Nylon shower curtains

Wash nylon shower curtains by hand and drip dry.

23 Perspiration marks

Soak in equal parts ammonia and water and add a little washing-up liquid overnight. Then wash as usual.

24 Plastic shower curtains/drapes

These stay soft and pliable if you add a few drops of mineral oil to rinse water after washing

25 Prevent deodorant stains on garments

Let deodorant dry fully before dressing.

Never leave stains: treat immediately.

Apply prewash spray or liquid detergent, then launder.

About every third washing, use hottest water safe for garment.

26 Rust and mineral stains

1 cup of bottled lemon juice in wash will remove marks from cotton.

27 Shirt collar stains

Paint hair shampoo into soiled areas before laundering.

28 Spaghetti stains

Wet fabric and sprinkle with powdered dish detergent. Brush gently with a toothbrush. Rinse and launder.

29 Travel stains

Keep a stain stick in your travel kit: use it before stains set so they wash out easily once home.

30 Tumble drying

Put delicate items in a pillow case.

31 Wardrobes and wash baskets

Put cotton balls sprayed with perfume or air freshener into corners and/or on shelves.

32 Washing blankets

These stay soft and fluffy if a little olive oil is added to final rinse.

33 Washing laundry costs less if you . . .

Use a lower wash temperature
AND/OR . . .
Use an economy wash
AND . . .
Do not underfill – always wash full loads.

34 Washing quilted or down duvets

Ensure no weak seams need attention. Spot-clean stains and wash in a gentle cycle with mild detergent. Rinse well. Tumble-dry until feathers fluff up. Placing knotted towels or tennis balls in dryer helps this.

THEN, IF POSSIBLE . . .

Air over a blanket outdoors in sunshine to bleach out remaining marks.

35 Washing synthetic blankets

Using a fabric softener reduces static and makes them softer.

36 Washing with baking soda

Use soda in the wash instead of proprietary softeners. It sweetens and softens the clothes well.

37 Whitening socks

Mix ½ cup liquid chlorine bleach, ½ cup automatic dishwasher detergent in 2 gallons water. Soak in this for 3½ hours.
OR . . .
Cream of Tartar will whiten fabrics too delicate for strong chemicals.

38 White-out and permanent marker stains

Apply sunscreen over stain and rub with a paper towel. Repeat as needed.

Pets & Pests

1   Ant deterrent

Draw a line with chalk wherever ants march. Ants do not like crossing it.

2   Ants invading pet food

Keep ants from your pet's dishes by wiping the floor under and around with a cloth dipped in kerosene.

AND/OR . . .

Stand food dish in a larger dish containing water.

3 Birdcages

Wipe over the inside with lemon juice. It acts as a safe disinfectant.

4 Cages

To prevent any curious youngster popping open the door to a pet cage or birdcage, secure this with a plastic bread clip.

5 Cat hairs

Some people have allergies to hairs and pet fleas. If animals have sneaked into the bedroom, put your pillows in a hot tumble dryer for 20 minutes. High temperatures will kill fleas.

6   Catching mice

Use fruit and nut chocolate as bait – or try tuna fish.

7   Cat tree for claws

Make a cat-tree so your new kitten scratches this instead of the furniture. Nail a log of firewood upright on a square of board and cover with carpet.

8   Chocolate trap

Bait a bottle with crumbled chocolate biscuit. Leave overnight with a ramp to provide mice with initial access. Once inside, the bottle's steep sides prevent escape.

9   Clothes moths

Moths love the scent of people so wash or dry-clean winter clothing before putting away.

AND . . .

Disguise scent by storing clothes with bunches of lavender.

OR . . .

Perfume clothes with genuine lavender oil before storing.

10   Cockroach/roach deterrent

Mix equal parts of sugar and boric acid (sold in hardware stores and chemists/drugstores). Sprinkle in crevices and, if building, between walls before putting up plasterboard. Put powder in jar lids behind the fridge and under sinks – but do keep mixture away from children and pets.

11 Company for a puppy

If you have to leave your puppy for a few hours put on the radio, so they will think people are still around.

12 Conventional mousetraps

Usually mice will run around room edges near to the skirting board so place the active part of the trap nearest to the wall.

13 Cushion protection

Mothballs in a cushion will keep the cat off the furniture.

14 Cushions

Use a damp sponge to remove dog or cat fur from cushions.

15 Dog dishes

Once empty, light dog plates can blow away if outside. Fill a container with sand and sit feeding bowl inside this.

16 Familiar smells

If your pet is going into kennels while you are away, tie a piece of your sock onto its collar. Your scent will reduce fretting.

17 Feeding young puppies

Young puppies enjoy lamb milk replacement available from local agricultural suppliers.

18 Fetching a ball

Use an old tennis racquet to hit the ball. It goes much further than you could throw it and improves the dog's exercise.

19 Flea collar that is too big for a kitten

To make an additional hole, heat a steel knitting needle and then push through.

20 Flea powder

Talcum powder is very effective and relatively harmless. Sprinkle into affected area.

21 Fleas

After combing, dip flea comb into a bowl of water and washing up liquid. The liquid film reduces surface tension so the fleas cannot escape once popped in.

22 Foil on seats

Cover chairs and tabletops with aluminium foil. Pets do not like the sound it makes – or the texture.

23 Fur balls

Put a little petroleum jelly on the pet's nose. When licked, it turns into mineral oil and helps shift fur balls.

24 Fussy eaters

At meal times, if your cat turns up its nose when you serve it canned food, try warming this for 10 seconds in the microwave.

25 Garbage bags

Sprinkle these with a little malt vinegar or pepper. Cats do not like these smells and will not tear open bags.

26 Healing oil

Apply tea-tree oil to small cuts and scratches: your pet will then leave the wound alone to heal.

27 Herbal litter

Crush herbs from the garden and mix in the litter to act as a deodoriser.

28 Hot weather

When out and about, carry a plastic shower cap in your pocket so you can fill it from a tap to quench your dog's thirst.

29 Keep cats away from garden

Dip cotton buds in eucalyptus oil and stick them in the soil.

30 Keeping drains clear

If your pet is moulting, cover drain-hole at bath-time with a strainer to prevent loose hairs blocking drains.

31   Keeping puppies cool

Freeze small bottles of water and put them in enclosure or garden. Puppies drape themselves over the bottles to stay cooler.

32   Keeping safe on the roads

If your dog or cat goes out at night, put reflector tape on its collar.

33   Kennels

Put your dog's kennel on wheels so it can be moved to prevent grass yellowing and can be rolled under cover in wet weather.

34   Kitten toys

Scrunched up aluminium makes a great toy ball.
OR . . .
Empty cotton spools can be chased around or suspended on string.
OR . . .
A big paper bag to dive inside provides lots of fun, especially with a ball to chase inside.

'Ping-pong' table tennis balls are light and fun to chase.

35   Knotted hair

If your dog's hair tangles easily, use a gentle conditioning rinse when he or she is bathed.

36 Mint fresh

Keep pet's drinking water fresh by adding a few crushed mint leaves. This also helps to prevent algae.

37 Paws

If your dog has to wear a bandage on a paw and keeps chewing this off, spread soap on it.

38   Pests at night

If your kitchen is being visited by mice or roaches, sprinkle flour around the edges of floor, cupboards, walls, windowsills and doors. Marks and trails will help you to locate their entry point or hiding place. Treat this area with a deterrent or block it up.

39   Puppy chewing

Dab oil of cloves onto legs of furniture.

40 Roaches

Place strong sticky tape to trap these pests where they roam. Most small household pests, such as roaches, find it impossible to escape once in contact with adhesive.

41 Scratching furniture

Place orange or lemon peel around or rub peel on to the surfaces. Cats and dogs do not like citrus smells.

42 Slugs

Catch slugs in a glass of beer sunk in the garden
OR . . .
Sprinkle bran around plants to deter them.
OR . . .
Surround precious young plants with sharp-edged broken pot pieces and egg shells.

43 Small household pests

These can be trapped on lengths of double-sided sticking tape, carpet tape or parcel tape. Stick to floor or apply tape to cardboard. Place tape or pads where pests track.

44 Smells

Bicarbonate of soda will deodorize carpets and upholstery and works well on pet smells. Sprinkle on with a flour sifter and vacuum away after 15 minutes.

45 Tar

Tar stuck on an animal's coat can be removed by rubbing eucalyptus oil into it. Leave for an hour, then shampoo out.

46 Teddy bears

These can carry dust mites, or pet's fleas or hairs. Put them into a hot tumble dryer for 20 minutes.

47 Teething toys

Discourage a puppy from chewing furniture by giving him a toy box with socks, slippers, ball, skipping rope, and so on.

48 Wasps

Half fill an old jam jar with ginger syrup and washing up liquid. The wasps will be attracted to the mixture and then trapped inside.

49 Weevils

Put a bay leaf in flour, corn meal, or other staples to keep weevils away.

AND . . .

Bay leaves in a cupboard will deter these pests.

50 Woodlice

Make a border of sticky tape to trap these pests. Woodlice find it impossible to escape once in contact with adhesive tape.

Health,
Beauty
&
Fashion Tips

1   Acne, blackheads, and pimples

Apply fresh mint juice over face nightly.

OR . . .

Mix lemon juice and rose water and leave on skin for ½ hour.

OR . . .

Crush 2 garlic cloves, and rub on the face twice a day, followed by lemon juice overnight. Wash off in morning.

2   Add height

Look taller by wearing one colour from head to toe. Choose a close-fitting shape, and avoid contrasting belts.

3 Adding shine to hair

Use dilute vinegar to final rinse.

4 Anaemia

Eat iron-rich foods like almonds, apples, apricots, bananas, beetroot, carrots, gooseberry, grapes, honey, lettuce, onion, pomegranate, raisins, salad leaves, spinach, tomatoes
AND . . .
Drink fresh apple juice an hour before meals or before going to bed.
ALSO . . .
Have a ripe banana with 1 tablespoon of honey, twice a day.

5   Animal bites

Mix castor oil and lime juice in equal amounts. Massage bite area with this.
ALSO . . .
Drink 1 cup warm water mixed with lime juice and honey.

6   An irritating mosquito bite

Apply lime juice diluted with water.

7   Antibiotic home remedy

Steep 3–4 garlic buds in brandy in the dark for 2 weeks. Take a few drops several times a day.

8   Arthritis

Eat fresh fish daily or take fish oil capsules.
AND . . .
Don't drink coffee.

9   Asthma

Before going to bed, take 1 teaspoon honey with
½ teaspoon cinnamon.
OR . . .
Steep 3–4 garlic buds in brandy in the dark for
2 weeks. Take a few drops several times a day.

10 Avoid static in lingerie

Choose natural fabric underwear or use generous amounts of fabric softener when washing lingerie.

11 Big boobs

Avoid tops with loud, bright prints. Keep heavy patterns to trousers and skirts.

12 Bladder stones

Drink a daily dose of 2 figs boiled in a cup of water – for a month.

13   Boosting energy levels

Simmer 1 cup honey and 3 cups water until $\frac{1}{4}$ evaporates. Strain and store in a dark bottle or crock. Cover with a cloth so it stays clean but can breathe. Keep cool. Add cinnamon, cloves, or lemon juice, if preferred.

14   Breath a little sour

Cinnamon boiled in a cup of water makes a good mouthwash.

OR . . .

Chew parsley leaves.

OR . . .

Chew cardamom seeds.

15 Bruises

Place a slice of raw onion over the bruise (but not on any broken skin).

16 Chapped hands

Use your face mask on your hands. This helps to keep your hands feeling soft and smooth. Avoid using clay or mud based masks.

OR . . .

Cover hands in vaseline/petroleum jelly and put plastic gloves over the top. Leave overnight if possible and wash off in the morning.

17 Chewing gum in hair:

Soak in coke®.

18 Circulatory problems

Take 2–3 teaspoon black strap molasses each day.

19 Classic clothing for travel

Choose simple, classic dresses – or mix and match tops, skirts and trousers – to dress up or down with jewellery, scarves, belts and so on for a wide range of effects.

20 Conditioning damaged, dry hair

Separate an egg. Whip white to a peak. Add 1 tablespoon water to yolk and blend until creamy. Then mix white and yolk together. Wet hair, remove excess moisture, and apply mixture to scalp. Massage gently, then rinse with cool water. Keep applying and rinsing until it is all gone.

21 Constipation in children

Soak 6–8 raisins in hot water: cool, crush well and strain.
ALSO . . .
Plenty of fresh fruit – and vegetables like carrots, cabbage, radish and spinach – will help.

22 Constipation

Take 1 teaspoon honey and juice of ½ a lemon in a glass of hot water first thing in the morning (this is an adult dose).

ALSO . . .

Drink 1 litre of water at breakfast.

AND . . .

Eat 300 grams of fresh grapes daily.

AND . . .

Eat liquorice sticks.

23 Coughs

Steep 3–4 garlic buds in brandy in the dark for 2 weeks. Take a few drops several times a day.

24 Cystitis or any bladder infection

Drink cranberry juice or make your own by boiling cranberries in water – do not add sugar.

25 Damage at the dry-cleaners

If a garment is damaged at the dry-cleaners and they claim it is not their fault, contact a fair trading office or equivalent.

26 Dandruff

Massage vinegar into scalp; leave for a few minutes. Then wash hair as normal. Repeat daily until dandruff disappears.

27 Dark circles around eyes

Make a paste with 1 teaspoon tomato juice, ½ teaspoon lemon juice, a pinch of turmeric powder and a teaspoon of flour. Apply and leave for 10 minutes; then wash off. Be careful not to get any into your eyes.

28 De-junk your wardrobe

Once or twice a year, throw out or give away clothes that you have not worn.

29 Deodorising feet

Brew 2 tea bags in $2^1/_2$ cups of water for 15 minutes and then put into 2 litres of cool water. Soak feet in strong tea for 20 minutes each day.

30 Diaper rash

Mix corn starch into a paste with water and apply to soothe.

31 Diarrhoea

Dissolve 4 grams of ground cinnamon in 1 cup of warm water, cover for 15 minutes; then drink.

32 Diarrhoea

Eat boiled sweet potatoes with salt and pepper before going to bed.

33 Dry cleaning

Always check care labels on new clothes before purchase. Dry-cleaning can be expensive.

34 Dry-cleaning delicate items

Always discuss any possible problems with the dry-cleaner first.

35 Dry-cleaning labels

Keep care labels on garments; they tell the dry-cleaner which solvents and temperatures to apply.

36 Dry elbows

Rub area with half a wedge of lemon. Then apply a moisturiser.

37 Dry or chapped hands

Use a hydrating face mask on your hands.

38 Dry skin

Mix 1 cup oatmeal, 1 cup warm water, 1 tablespoon vanilla extract and $1/2$ cup baking soda to a smooth paste. Pour paste under running water while filling bath. A good soak in this relieves dry, itchy skin.

39 Earache

Steep 2 teaspoons of chamomile flowers in boiling water for 15 minutes. Strain and apply on a cloth to relieve earache.

40 Eczema

Make a paste with nutmeg in a little water (or in saliva). Apply to affected areas.

41 Emphasise necklines

To compliment a long neck, choose V-necks and plunging necklines in darker clothes which highlight skin tones.

42 Eye lotion

Simmer 1 cup water and 1 teaspoon honey for 5 minutes. Dip a cloth into liquid and apply to closed eye.

43 Facial cleanser

Mix 2 tablespoon corn starch, 2 tablespoon glycerin, and ½ cup water until smooth. Heat in a small container in a saucepan of hot water until thick and clear. Do not boil. When cool, use instead of soap.

44 Flatulence

Dissolve 4 grams of ground cinnamon in 1 cup of warm water, cover for 15 minutes; then drink.

45   Gym membership

Gyms and sports clubs can go bust. Pay per visit or join one that offers membership on a one-to-three month basis.

46   Hair tongs

Make a case for these from a kitchen pot holder. Fold in half and sew the outside edges, leaving one small side open. This makes a handy heat-proof case when you travel away.

47 Handbag care

Keep bags out of direct sunlight.

AND . . .

Fill bags with crumpled newspaper when not in use.

AND . . .

Store in a soft cloth bag or an old pillow case.

48 Hand-washing woollens

Do not let water from the tap pour directly onto woollens: this can matt the fibres.

49 Hangover relief

Keep drinking plenty of fluid to flush out the alcohol.

AND . . .

Eat honey on crackers. The fructose helps to flush the alcohol from your system.

50 Hay fever

Steep 1 teaspoon fenugreek seed in 1 cup water. Leave, covered, for 10 minutes. Drinking 1 cup a day relieves symptoms.

51 Headache

Eat a dozen almonds.

52 Hiccups

Plug both ears, and then very slowly swallow a mouthful of water.

53 Hickey (love bites)

Coat area with lotion. Rub vigorously with the back of a cold spoon, changing to new cold spoon every 10 minutes. Continue for an hour if possible.

54 Hiding panty line

Wear stretch cotton G-strings or figure-hugging briefs or hosiery under slim-fitting clothes.

55 Insect bites

Mix corn starch into a paste with water and apply to draw out the poisons.

56 Jackets

Do not unpick hidden stitching in pockets: jacket will keep its shape longer.

57 Jewelry freshen-up

Rings and earrings can be cleaned and polished at the jewelers.

OR . . .

Soak for a few minutes in undiluted washing up liquid, then rinse.

58 Keeping suede shoes in shape

Scotchgard suede or nubuck shoes and boots before wearing them in wet weather.

59 Kidney problems

Drink cranberry juice or make your own by boiling cranberries in water – without sugar.

60 Lightening hair

Place ¼ cup chopped fresh rhubarb in 2 cups boiling water: cool, strain, and use as a rinse.
AND/OR . . .
Sit in bright sunlight, especially straight from the pool.

61 Lingerie care

Wash and tumble dry bras, pants and delicate items in cloth lingerie bags.

62 Lipstick stains

Dab on surgical spirit or methylated spirits/ denatured alcohol first, then wash normally.

63 Looking slimmer

Wear darker colours (black, navy and deep brown)

AND . . .

Wear one colour from top to toe.

64 Looks like new

Bring new life to your old favourites by dyeing clothes or having this done professionally – great for jeans.

65 Maximising sales and special offers

Check through your wardrobe and list real needs in order of importance.

66 Morning sickness

Use 1 teaspoon each of fresh juice of mint and lime, with 1 tablespoon honey. Mix and take 3 times a day.

AND . . .

Get up slowly.

AND . . .

Nibble at dry crackers at regular intervals.

67 Mosquito bites

Relieve itch by rubbing soap on the area.

68 Mosquito repellent

Avoid bites by taking vitamin B yeast tablets (or Marmite) for 3 weeks prior to travel and then when away. The yeast in your perspiration repels biting insects.

69 Mosquito repellent

Avon Skin-so-Soft bath oil seems to repel mosquitoes though no one knows why!

70 Mucus in cough

Pour 1 cup boiling water over $\frac{1}{2}$ teaspoon each of cinnamon, ginger and ground cloves. Filter; then sweeten with honey and drink.

71 Muscle cramps

Apply clove oil on affected areas.

72 Natural pain relief

Honey is natural antidote to pain. Drink 3 tablespoons in boiled water.

73 Nausea

Boil $1/2$ cup of rice in 1 cup of water for about 15 minutes. Drain into a cup and sip.

74 New buttons

Update a classic garment or suit by sewing on new buttons.

AND . . .

A change to good quality buttons on a new garment can make it look more expensive.

75 New jewelry for old

Remember that a good jeweler can remake pieces into something different.

76 Obesity

Mix lime juice with honey and water. Drink every morning.

OR . . .

Mix 3 teaspoon lime juice, ¼ teaspoon black pepper, 1 teaspoon honey, and 1 cup water; drink daily for 3 months

OR . . .

Mix 1 teaspoon lime juice with 1 cup water and drink each morning.

OR . . .

Eat a tomato before breakfast.

77 Oily skin

Make a paste with $\frac{1}{2}$ cup cooked oatmeal, 1 egg white, 1 tablespoon lemon juice, and $\frac{1}{2}$ cup mashed apple. Apply to face and leave for 15 minutes before rinsing.

78 Out of breath with hiccups

Drink $\frac{1}{2}$ glass water very slowly.
OR . . .
Suck a teaspoon of sugar slowly.
OR . . .
Suck 2–3 small pieces of fresh ginger.

79 Out of earshot

Warmed glycerine may relieve congested wax in ear.

80 Out of season coats

Check for loose hems, then dry-clean and leave in dry-cleaning bags until needed again.

81 Overweight

To reduce fat intake, drink up to 3 cups of green tea daily.

82 Packing shoes

Fill shoes with socks or pants and pack them in plastic bags or shoe bags. They will keep their shape, space is saved, and your other clothes are protected from dirty soles.

83 Pantihose

Prevent ladders running by dabbing a small amount of clear nail polish onto a tear.

84 Recycle fashions

Revamp by changing collars, reshaping loose garments and chopping long pants into shorter styles.

85 Relieving depression

³⁄₄ cup of cooked spinach a day will boost vitamin levels.

86 Removing dust or lint

Use a clothes brush
OR . . .
Masking tape, wrapped around your hand, will work.

87 Resistant acne

Add 3 teaspoonfuls of dried basil leaves to 1 cup boiling water. Leave for 15 minutes. Cool and apply with cotton ball.

88 Savoury treatment for bad colds or flu

Sauté 6 chopped cloves of garlic in oil. Add a quart of stock and boil for a few seconds. Lower heat. Separate 2 eggs: stir whites into liquid. Mix yolks with 2 tablespoon of vinegar and add. Use salt and pepper to taste.

89 Scarves

Hang scarves over a coat-hanger to lessen creasing.

90 Shoe repairs

Each autumn/fall and spring, organise repairs, resoling, cleaning, dyeing and so on so – when you do not need to wear your favorites.

91 Skin tonic

Mix and stir well 2 tablespoons vodka, 1½ teaspoon honey and 1 tablespoon fennel seeds. Leave for 3 days. Strain and either use at full strength or add 2 tablespoons water to dilute. Apply to face with a cotton ball.

92 Small cosmetic items

Fix a magnetic strip to the inside of your medicine cabinet door. Then tweezers, nail clippers, or small scissors will be easy to find.

93 Soap leftovers

Mix soap slivers with some water in a blender to make your own liquid soap. Try adding a little glycerine.

94 Softening your skin

Add powdered milk to your bathwater. The lactic acid helps remove dead skin cells and improves skin tones.

95 Soothing a sore throat

Mix 1 tablespoon honey and 1 teaspoon lime juice. Slowly swallow small amounts 2–3 times daily.

96 Sore mouth

Drink peppermint tea: it is an antiseptic and contains menthol which relieves pain. Boil 5 grams of fresh peppermint in 1 cup of water. Add a little salt.

97 Splinters

Soak skin in vegetable oil for a few minutes. Then remove splinter with tweezers.

OR . . .

Place scotch tape over splinter and then rip off again.

AND/OR . . .

Place an ice cube on to the area. This will help to reduce swelling and numb the pain, making removal much easier.

98 Stomach pain

Dissolve 4 grams of ground cinnamon in 1 cup of warm water, cover for 15 minutes; then drink.

99 Stop smoking

When you have the urge to smoke, dip the tip of your tongue into a little salt.

100 Stopping hiccups

Suck hard on a sugar cube or a wedge of lemon.

OR . . .

Hold an ice cube against the side of your neck.

101 Storing clean pantihose

Prevent snagging by rolling them into a ball and tying before storing in drawers.

102 Strengthening weak nails

Mix well 2 teaspoons of salt, 2 teaspoons castor oil, and 1 teaspoon wheatgerm oil. Keep in a bottle. Shake and then rub a small amount into nails, leave for 4 minutes and wipe off. Apply more plain castor oil: this also makes nails shine.

103 Suit hangers

Good suit hangers are an excellent investment and will keep jackets, coats and tailored clothes in much better shape.

104 Sunburn

Mix 4 tablespoon buttermilk and 2 teaspoon tomato juice. Leave on sore areas for $1/2$ hour.
OR . . .
Camomile lotion is good at relieving soreness.

105 Thick waist

Choose loose-fitting tops that come to the hips, and avoid tucking in.

106 Think accessories

Invest in good accessories: they lift an outfit and stay in fashion far longer than do garments.

107 Throbbing headache

Cut a lime in half and rub it on your forehead.

108 Ties

A man's tie looks neatest if the tip just touches the belt buckle.

109 Tight tops and clinging T-shirts

Wear a flesh-coloured, seamless bra for a smooth look.

110 Tiredness

Grapefruit and lemon juice mixed in equal parts relieves fatigue.

111 Toothache

Drink peppermint tea: it is an antiseptic and contains menthol which relieves pain. Boil 5 grams of fresh peppermint in 1 cup of water. Add a little salt.

112 Toothpicks

Store these in a parmesan cheese shaker.

113 Trainers and beach shoes

Remove laces and inner soles, spray with a stain remover and then machine wash with a biological detergent. Dry away from direct sunlight.

114 Travel tip

Avoid linen and 100 per cent cotton; they crease.

115 Use your mirror

Always check your appearance from all angles in a *full-length* mirror.

116 Varicose veins

Take 2–3 teaspoon black strap molasses each day.

117 Vomiting and nausea

Suck a piece of ice.

AND/OR . . .

Eat ½ teaspoon ground cumin seeds.

ALSO . . .

Cinnamon and sliced ginger interrupt nausea signals sent from stomach to brain. Sprinkle cinnamon into a herbal tea or simmer a few slices of ginger in hot tea water.

118 Warts

Protect skin around wart with petroleum jelly. Then tape a slice of garlic to wart.

119 Washing knitwear

This can stretch on hangers. Dry laid out flat.

120 Wet shoes

Dry out by stuffing them with crumpled newspaper, then dry slowly, out of direct sunlight.

121 Whitening teeth

Mix salt with finely powdered rind of lime. Use this as toothpowder frequently.

122 Wise investment

Buy classic styles rather than extreme fashion fads.

123 Woollens and knitwear

When ironing, place a damp cloth on top of woollens and knitwear before pressing. Do not push iron or garment may pull out of shape.

124 Wrinkles

Mix and stir well 2 tablespoons vodka, 1½ teaspoon honey and 1 tablespoon fennel seeds. Leave for 3 days. Strain and either use at full strength or add 2 tablespoons water to dilute. Apply to face with a cotton ball.

AND . . .

Apply coconut oil to skin and gently massage skin before retiring for the night.

Gardening

1   Ant invasion in pots

Soak pots then lift out plants and remove nests at the base. Repot and place on bricks regularly cleaned with eucalyptus oil.

AND . . .

Put a ring of white pepper around the pot.

2   Ants in garden

Sprinkle talcum powder and white pepper into paving crevices or wherever ants invade.

3   Aphids

Aphids are attracted to yellow. Trap them in a bowl of detergent containing a few drops of yellow food colour with cooking oil floating on it.

AND . . .

Spray infested plants with diluted washing up fluid.

4   Automatic watering

Installing a permanent watering system available from garden centres or by mail order to save hours of watering hanging baskets.

5 Avocado seeds

In late summer, an avocado seed can be planted in potting mix, and left in shade until it germinates. It will make an attractive houseplant.

6 Barbecue firelighters

Used dried citrus skins as firelighters. The oil burns well and smells lovely.

7   Barbecue plates

Use big banana leaves for plates and serve fruit salad in a hollowed-out melon. Sorbet can be served in hollowed-out lemon or orange skins or in pineapple shells with fruit and cheese on vine leaves or young greens or cabbage leaves. It is eco-friendly and looks great.

8   Black-spot on roses

Water roses in the morning so they are not wet all night: moisture encourages Black-spot. Mow surrounding lawn often as Black-spot likes long grass.

9   Bulbs

Invest in spring bulbs for early colour. Do feed them well after they have flowered to ensure a good show in successive years.

10   Colour co-ordination

Buy pots in similar colour tones for a professional look.

11   Cactus

Cactus need minimal maintenance and children enjoy growing these but must be warned not to touch the spines.

12 Camellias

(and other flowers that tend to droop)
If cutting for indoors, crisscross vase top with strips of sticky tape to hold flowers in place.
OR . . .
Float camellias in shallow bowls.

13 Cat deterrent

Keep cats out of the children's sandpits and off seedlings by draping these with bird netting.

14 Citrus skins

Dry the fragrant peel and crumble them into powder for flavouring in cooking.

15 Clubs

Join a local gardening club to share ideas and buy gardening supplies at wholesale prices.

16 Daffodils

Make a pot of daffodils last longer by keeping cool. Plant in big pots and keep away from bright sunshine or hot places.

17 Dead-heading

Prune dead flowers regularly to encourage more blooms and discourage disease.

18 Decking

Scrub stains and algae away with laundry bleach.

19 Delphiniums

Delphinium seeds should be planted immediately as they need to be really fresh to germinate. If you can collect your own from existing plants, so much the better.

20 Difficult soil

If soil is heavy clay and/or waterlogged, build raised beds and fill with new soil or compost.

21 Dried flowers

Dry flowers for winter by placing them on a layer
of borax or silica gel in a shoe box.

OR . . .

Hang upside down in an airy position away from
direct light.

22 Drying herbs

Collect a few leaves each week of mint,
rosemary, golden marjoram, thyme or whatever
grows in your garden in summer. Place in a
warm place to dry (or microwave for just a few
seconds). Then chop or mince and store for
winter use.

23 Dust pests

If you have saw-fly larvae that eat pear, cherry and hawthorn leaves – dust these with vacuum cleaner residue. If you can blow it out directly, it will go higher up the tree. The dry dust dehydrates the larvae.

24 Easy plants

Agapanthus blooms in shade or sun, in exposed places, in sea air, and on clay or sandy soil.

25 Feeding baskets and tubs

All containers need lots of feeding but take the chore out of this by inserting slow-release capsules that last all summer.

26 Ferns

Indoor ferns turn brown if the air is too dry –
they thrive in steamy bathrooms.

27 Flower water

Collect lavender heads and just cover with hot
white wine vinegar.

OR . . .

Cover rose petals with vodka. Leave for a week,
add fresh flowers – leave again, then strain and
add an equal volume of mineral water. Spray on
as a scent.

28 Fly trap

A jar of fruit juice with a pinch of yeast added, and a teaspoon of cooking oil on top will attract and trap vinegar or ferment flies.

29 Fresh pots

Paint old tin pots and terracotta ones with your own designs for a fresh look.

30 Front doors

Keep two big pots of flowers on either side of the front door, appropriate to the season, for a warm welcoming look.

31 Garden paths

If planning a garden, build ramps instead of steps so that using a wheelbarrow is easier.

32 Garden sharing

Always share packets of seeds with a gardening friend, or agree to share produce for greater variety.

33 Garlic

Plant garlic cloves around plants susceptible to black spot and other leaf diseases. They also provide masses of flowers in midsummer.

34 Geraniums

These will not over-winter outside and must be kept indoors until frosts pass. They bloom continuously through summer and are excellent value for money. Cuttings take easily too.

35 Germinating seeds indoors

Put seeds in small containers in a warm spot, say, on a shelf above a radiator, and then move somewhere light and cool once seeds germinate.

36 Germinating seeds outdoors

In hot weather cover the seed bed with a few sheets of damp newspaper. Check every day and remove once seeds germinate.

37 Greasy barbecues

Scrape away the worst. Wash with very hot soapy water. Then use a mix of caustic soda and water if needed.

38 Green tomatoes

Use unripened green tomatoes to make chutney or relish.

OR . . .

Fry thin slices in batter.

OR . . .

Leave on a windowsill or somewhere warm to ripen indoors.

39 Greenhouses

Sweet basil and marigolds grown in a greenhouse will keep white fly away.

40 Hardy roses

Easy roses that need little pruning or spraying include Rugosas and old-fashioned roses such as climbing Albertine and Mermaid.

41 Help during vacation

Place pot plants in shade or under a tree. Ask a neighbour to help and make the task easier by keeping as many as possible grouped together within hosepipe reach.

42 Herb baskets

A hanging basket can be planted with herbs such as trailing thyme, garlic chives and parsley plants.

43 Herbs

Harvest basil and tarragon and cover with olive oil or boiling vinegar to keep the flavour through the cold months.

OR . . .

Make lots of pesto with your basil, then freeze it.

OR . . .

Wash tarragon leaves, then slip them into freezer bags, a few at a time, and freeze.

44 Indoor leaf care

Wipe your indoor plants once a week with a damp cloth. It keeps the leaves glossy and deters pests.

45 Indoor plants

Keep a water sprayer handy for quick freshening up of leaves and to remind you to water properly.

46 Insect pests

Try vacuuming up the larger ones from shrubs or fruit trees.

47 Kneepads

The kneepads teenagers use for in-line skating provide good knee protection that moves with you round the garden effortlessly.

48 Lawns

Feed a lawn frequently: well-fed lawns stay greener.

49 Leaky guttering

Clean around hole, lay epoxy filler over it according to the manufacturer's directions, then lay a piece of glass fibre mesh or fly wire over the hole and press it into filler. When this is dry, layer more filler on top and under hole.

50 Margarine tubs

These make good small seed trays when sowing. Keep lids for bases for watering and use clear lids or plastic on top to retain moisture until seeds germinate.

51 Massage oil

Place 2 chillies and a bunch of mint leaves in a jar with olive oil. Leave for three weeks, then strain to make a warming oil for winter.

52 Millipedes

Keep millipedes out of the house with a line of talcum power: they won't cross it!

53 Miniature greenhouses

Slice the tops off old plastic bottles and place over cuttings or seedlings. This deters pests, keeps the plant warm and, as the moisture condenses, waters them.

54 Mint

If you keep mint on your windowsill, make sure it is a rust-free kind. Apple mint is hardy on a sunny windowsill and is good chopped in fruit salad, in drinks, or in mint sauce.

55 Mould on paving

Scrub with toothbrush or steel wool and baking powder.

56 Moss

Use about 35–40g of iron sulphate (ferrous sulphate) per square metre or yard of lawn.

57 Mossy paths

Mossy paths can be slippery. Kill by spraying with one part methylated spirits/denatured alcohol and one part vinegar. Leave for 15 minutes, respray, then leave until dry. Rake or sweep off moss.

58 Mulch

To give the garden a fast 'face-lift', cover the soil between plants with bark or mulch.

59 Newspaper paths

Make paths between your plants or vegetables with old newspapers. Leave weeds here and then paper and weeds will rot down to make a good mulch.

60 Night tasks

Water late at night when the soil is cooler.

61 Old china

A potted plant will look good housed in a pretty teapot while old saucers make excellent stands for plant pots.

62 Old mosquito nets

Drape these over vegetables to keep cabbage white butterflies away.

AND . . .

Spread over stakes above tender seedlings in hot weather. The slight shade will help prevent wilting and keeps birds at bay.

63 Patio beans

Smaller sized runner beans grow well in baskets, too.

64 Patio fruits

Large pots or half barrels can serve as containers for small fruit trees like cumquats; for dwarf apples, peaches or nectarines; and lemons or grapefruit.

65 Patio paving

Fill all the cracks in your paving with alyssum seedlings. They'll look good – and choke out weeds. Land cress does well, too.

66 Patio potatoes

Take a large pot or strawberry pot, put in layers of potting mix, and seed potatoes. Keep topping it up with potting mix when potatoes grow, so only the top leaves show.

67 Patio rhubarb

Rhubarb will grow in a hanging basket by the backdoor. Plant a variety with thin red stems then pick, feed and water frequently.

68 Patio strawberries

Plant in a hanging basket for pretty flowers and attractive fruit.

69   Patio tomatoes

Certain cherry tomatoes will grow very well in a hanging basket.

70   Perlite and water retention capsules

Use these in tubs and baskets to maximise the water's effect and keep weight down.

71   Pots and baskets

For instant effect, invest in a few big pots and/or hanging baskets and fill with easy annuals for summer and pansies or primulas and ivies in winter.

72 Potted vegetables

Fill a good sized pot or grow-bag with lettuce plants (outside) and cucumbers and tomatoes (in a greenhouse) if you have no room for a vegetable plot.

73 Propagators

Styrofoam fruit boxes make excellent seed propagators but make sure there are holes in the bottom for drainage.

74 Protecting outdoor seeds

Roll vulnerable seeds in dried old tea leaves and white pepper, with a little oil. This will protect them from hungry mice or other pests and from rotting if the soil is cold.

75 Pruning trees and roses

Invest in good shears and secateurs and prune away dead wood or straggly branches.

76 Recycle plant pots

Wash in a dilute bleach solution to kill any germs, rinse well and use again.

77 Reservoirs

Either buy hanging baskets with a built-in reservoir or make a good layer of gravel at the base to improve water retention.

78 Rosemary firelighters

If pruning rosemary, keep the branches for your next barbecue. It crackles well and the aromatic smoke adds an extra element to your evening.

79 Save money

Take cuttings. Even if only a few succeed you will have saved precious spending and can swap any 'overs' with other gardening friends.

80 Saving seeds

Collect seeds from flowers and vegetables, such as poppies, wallflowers and tomatoes and plant the following spring.

81 Saving seeds safely

Empty plastic film canisters can keep seeds dry and safe. Label them carefully with flower type and date.

82 Seed collector

Slip an old pantihose leg over the seed head while the seeds ripen and when they fall they'll collect in the toe. You can then hang the seeds somewhere cool and dry until you need them.

83 Seed cups

Plastic drinking mugs pierced at the base make good pots for starting off sweet peas or sunflower seeds as they provide longer room for roots than do small round pots.

84 Shade-loving plants

These include agapanthus, bluebells, bugloss, camellias, daphne, ferns, hostas, impatiens, lilies, ornamental nettles, violets and variegated ivies.

85 Sheets and linen

Harvest your herb garden for pepper, cloves, bay leaves and lavender flowers. Combine with rock salt and then sew into small bags to keep your linen store smelling fresh.

86 Small advertisements

Check gardening magazines for useful suppliers of everything from pots to fences.

87 Small gardens

Use a trellis and/or pergola to extend your garden upwards.

88 Small space savouries

Plant onion chives and garlic chives, rhubarb, lovage, wild rocket, land cress and hardier tomatoes in tubs. Feed, weed, and water and enjoy!

89 Smother weeds

Forget about weeding – just mulch. This will smother the weeds.

90   Snail pellets

Protect pets and children from poisonous snail pellets by putting these in an old plastic container and taping the lid down. Cut two small holes at the bottom for the snails to gain access.

OR . . .

Hide the pellets under terracotta pots raised up on a stone.

91   Soap holder

Slip a piece of soap into the toe of old pantihose and tie to the hose fitting. You will always be able to find it, birds and mice won't be able to eat it – and the slightly abrasive pantihose will help clean the grime off your hands.

92 Spread enjoyment

Treat yourself to a packet of seeds, and then a new shrub or plant at regular intervals. It is easier to manage and spreads the budget.

93 Stakes

Old pantihose make excellent ties for plants – less likely to damage soft wood than rope or string.

94 Sun-loving plants

Always check the label before planting. If the plant needs full sun, make sure it has this. If it is in a pot in a shadier garden, it can be moved around through the day to maximize light intake.

95 Tall bins

Long narrow kitchen bins make good containers for roses or climbers that like a deep root run.

96 Thyme

Top-dress thyme bushes every year with good soil or compost. If they get leggy, cover with soil and new little roots will soon push through.

97 Tin can pots

Pierce a few holes in a big tin can, fill with potting compost, plant up and nail to a post.

98 Watering daily

Early morning is a good time to water but in hot dry weather, water at night, too – the moisture will soak in better and there is less risk of hot sun blanching wet leaves.

99 Weedkiller

Next time you boil the kettle, pour some boiling water onto a weed. It will wilt immediately.

100 Winter colour

Plant winter pansies, snowdrops, aconites and hellebores.

101 Yellow leaves

The plant may simply need feeding but always check for sap-sucking mites, or white, brown or greyish scales. Treat with an oil spray from your garden supplier.

Sense, Safety
&
Taking Care

1   Acid stomach

Take coconut water 3–4 times daily.

AND/OR . . .

Eat a generous slice of watermelon and/or some cucumber once an hour.

2   A jammed ring

If rings get wedged on fingers . . .

Use washing up liquid as a lubricant.

AND/OR . . .

Immerse hands in cold water and then try again.

OR . . .

Lubricate hands with cooking or olive oil.

3   Broken glass

Pick up fragments safely with a wedge of bread.

4   Broken light bulb

A light bulb broken in its socket can be difficult to unscrew. Jam a bar of soap, a piece of raw potato or a large cork into the base of the bulb and then twist out safely.

5   Bruises

Bathe in chilled hazel or arnica tincture.
Bromelain tablets reduce fluid build-up and swelling and relieve pain.

6   Burns

Hold a bag of ice (or frozen peas!) against burn to stop blistering. Split an aloe vera leaf and apply its gel to help healing.

7   Catarrh

Add a tablespoon of apple cider vinegar to a glass of warm water and sip.

8   Cold sores

If sore is dry, dab with drops of St John's Wort oil. If weeping, strain lemon balm tea and apply with a cotton bud.

9   Colds and flu

Take Echinacea tablets 3 times day at the first sign of a cold to boost the immune system.

OR . . .

Put 10 drops of liquid echinacea into a teaspoon of honey and lemon and hot water for flu remedy, take 3 times a day.

10   Constipation

Mix ½ cup each of chopped dried figs, pearl barley and raisins with a ¼ cup of chopped liquorice root and 1 litre of water. Boil and simmer, covered, for 30 minutes. Strain and keep in a bottle in fridge. Take 1 tablespoon.

11 Cough relief

Chop 3 cloves of garlic and 1 onion. Place in a bowl, cover with honey, leave for 3 hours and strain. Sip teaspoonful regularly for 1 day.

12 Cramps

Place a camphor block under the mattress
AND . . .
Mix 6 drops each of rosemary and clove oil with 30ml vegetable oil. Shake well, and massage muscle with it as needed.

13 Cut-out safety switches

Organise an electrician to install a safety cut-out switch to prevent electrocution.

14 Cuts

Unprocessed honey contains a natural antibiotic and is effective against infection.

15 Cystitis

Parsley is a natural diuretic and fights infection. Heat parsley in water in a covered pan to boiling point. Cool and add a few drops of lavender oil. Soak a cotton pad in water and hold against vagina to relieve burning feeling.

16 Dandruff

Mix 1 tablespoon each of dried rosemary and nettles with 2 cups of apple cider vinegar. Boil, remove from heat, cover, and leave overnight. Strain. After shampooing and rinsing hair, pour this over hair and leave to dry naturally.

17 Deodorising feet

Give feet a daily soak in strong tea for 15 minutes.

18 Diarrhoea

Peel and grate an apple into a bowl. Eat 15 minutes later when it is brown.

19   Do-it-yourself deodorant

Add 2 drops each of rosemary, cypress, and lemon with 8 drops each of cedar wood and patchouli essential oils to 125ml of distilled witch-hazel.

20   Dry cracked hands

Massage cold cooked mashed potato and olive oil into skin, leave for 10 minutes, and rinse.

21   Dry skin

Add 1 tablespoon of finely ground oatmeal to a bowl of warm water and rinse face and neck with this.

22 Earache

Crush 2 cloves of garlic into tablespoons of olive oil and warm gently over low heat. Strain. Ensure cool enough and then drip a few drops into ear; plug with cotton wad . Do not attempt this if there is any discharge or if eardrum might be perforated.

23 Earache

Heat sea salt in a heavy pan. Pour into a clean, cotton sock, leaving it pliable, like a beanbag. Tie end. Apply for 30 minutes.

24 Emergency rain cover

In case you forget your raincoat or the weather changes suddenly, keep a new plastic garbage bag in the car. Cut a hole in the bottom for your head and side openings for your arms. It will protect you and your clothing.

25 Fatigue

Blend 15 drops of may chang (Litsea cubeba) with 10 drops of marjoram and 5 drops of peppermint oil in 30ml of almond oil. Put drops on a tissue and inhale.

AND . . .

Take Siberian ginseng.

26 Fire extinguisher

Always keep baking soda in the car as this will put out a fire.

27 Fluid retention before periods

Take 3 cups of dandelion tea each day in week prior to menstruation.

28 Haemorrhoids

Saturate a cotton ball with distilled witch hazel and apply several times a day.

29 Head lice

Add 10 drops of thyme essential oil to 1 teaspoon of shampoo. Mix well and apply to scalp and hair. Leave 5 minutes then rinse well with a 50/50 mix of apple cider vinegar and water. Use with caution; never apply undiluted.

30 Improve poor circulation

Add 1 tablespoon of dried mustard to a bowl of hot water and soak feet.

31 Indigestion

Peel and grate a small piece of fresh root ginger into a cup. Add boiling water and steep for 5 minutes. Strain, sweeten with honey and drink.
AND . . .
Take Swedish bitters before a meal.

32 Insomnia

Add 2 cups of Epsom salts to your bath to relax muscles.
AND . . .
Add 1 teaspoon of dried passionflower to 1 cup of boiling water; steep for 15 minutes. Drink 1 hour before bed.

33 Itching insect bites

Apply one drop of peppermint oil to bite.

34 Lightning

Never unplug equipment during a thunderstorm, especially if it is connected to an external aerial. A high static charge can build up on the aerial and cable even if the storm is several miles away.

35 Menstruation cramps

Mix 4 drops of clary sage oil into 2 teaspoons of almond oil, Massage over lower abdomen.

36 Morning sickness

Simmer peeled fresh ginger root and cinnamon. Add honey and lemon, and drink.

OR . . .

Drink raspberry leaf tea.

37 Mouth ulcers

Steep 2 tablespoons of dried sage in very hot water for 15 minutes. Strain; add 3 drops of myrrh essential oil and shake well Gargle frequently.

38 Muscle pain

Heat sea salt in a heavy pan. Pour into a clean, cotton sock, leaving it pliable, like a beanbag. Tie end. Apply to painful area for 30 minutes.

39 Nappy/diaper rash

Add strong, strained chamomile tea to bath water.

AND . . .

Wipe bottom with cod liver oil between nappy/diaper changes.

40 Pimples

Dab on toothpaste each night.
OR . . .
Apply tea-tree or lavender oil.

41 Rash after shaving

Apply cold wet chamomile tea bags.
OR . . .
Dip a cloth into strained, cool chamomile tea
and press over rash.
OR . . .
Apply aloe vera gel.

42 Reducing colds and flu symptoms

Take Echinacea

OR . . .

Try tincture or tablets of astragalus, a Chinese herb.

OR . . .

Take ginger-garlic tea made from 1 teaspoon of grated ginger in 1 cup of water, left covered for 5 minutes. Strain and add 1 crushed garlic clove, 1 tablespoon fresh lemon juice, and ¼ teaspoon cayenne powder. Sweeten with honey.

43 Relieving chickenpox itch

Grind dry rolled oats to make a fine powder. Bathe patient in a bath with two cups of the mix added to lukewarm water.

44   Relieving colic

Drink peppermint tea –pour 1 cup of boiling water over 2 teaspoons of dried peppermint leaves. Cover and leave for 15 minutes. Strain. Use ½ a teaspoonful as often as needed.

45   Seasickness

Eat dry crackers at regular intervals.
AND . . .
Keep the horizon in view.

46   Sinus headache

Eat seeded chillies to loosen congestion and relieve pain.

47 Sinusitis relief

Mix 1 teaspoon of finely grated horseradish with apple cider vinegar and honey, and then inhale to open sinuses.

48 Solvent based paint

This should never be poured down drains. It needs to be disposed of as a household hazardous waste. Contact the local Council or State Government Environmental Protection Agency for advice or collection details.

49 Sore eyes

Add 2 drops each of chamomile and lavender essential oils to a cup of spring water. Mix well. Soak 2 cotton pads in liquid, squeeze out excess and place a pad over each eye. Lie down with feet higher than head.

AND . . .

Take bilberry tablets.

50 Stained teeth

Crush a strawberry and rub the pulp onto teeth; then rinse. Tea and coffee stains vanish.

51 Stressed out

Valerian helps relaxation. Drink as a tea or take as capsules.

52 Swimming pool cleaning

Baking soda with bleach will keep pools clean and hygienic.

53 Swimming pool safety

Never leave children unattended in or near a pool.

54 Thrush

Buy marigold tea from a health food store. Steep for 10 minutes, strain and cool. Add 4 drops of lavender oil and then bathe affected area.

55 Toothache

Chew 2 cloves.

OR . . .

Apply cotton soaked in clove oil to tooth and gum.

56 Warts

Sprinkle chopped fresh pineapple with salt and leave overnight in bowl. Strain off juice and store in fridge. Dab warts 3 times daily.

Craftwork

1   Acrylic painting tip

Acrylic paints dry darker. If they need lightening, try a wash of soft white and cream over the top.

22   Baby mementoes

Cover a shoe box and use to store baby's hospital name tag, first photographs, and so on.

3   Bees wax candles

If using bees wax sheets when candle making, stop them sticking to themselves by using cookie cutters, then pressing them to the candles.

4   Bobbin tangles

Use plumber's tape to secure bobbin threads and prevent tangles..

5   Buttonholes

Apply patches of sticky tape where you are making buttonholes. Work buttonholes over tape; remove when complete.

6   Buttons

Select good buttons to make a new garment truly individual or to perk up an old one.

7 Candle making

In an old saucepan melt down old candle stubs. Remove any wicking. Tint molten wax with candle dyes and then pour into prepared moulds.

8 Candle making molds

Leftover milk and drink cartons and plumbing pipe sections make excellent molds.

9 Complicated cross-stitch patterns

Mark material in grids of 10, in cotton. Start work from the middle of the grid.

10 Covering buttons

Covering buttons with matching fabric gives a fine tailored effect.

11 Cutting dressmaking patterns

Always cut around all the markings and use the sharpest scissors possible.

12 Cutting out around paper patterns

Sharp prinking shears keep fraying to a minimum

13 Decoupage images

When cutting paper images, move the paper into the blades of the scissors to produce a smooth bevelled edge-finish on the paper.

14 Decoupage

Wait for a fine, dry day to apply varnish layers. If the air is moist, the surface may cloud.

15 Do not fold

Never leave your sewing work folded: creases can be hard to remove later and soon collect dirt.

16 Emergency hemming

Keep sticky hemming fabric in your haberdashery cupboard for quick rescue operations.

17 Ensure good light for sewing

Buy a daylight bulb or sit in daylight, to ease eye strain and make identifying colours easier.

18 Fabric like velvet, with a pile

Always check pile runs the same way. Cut out in good daylight to be sure.

16 Fingerprints in clay

Wear disposable plastic gloves when you are working with modeling clay to avoid finger prints.

20 Gift boxes

Add fake flowers and lace or ribbon to make a box lid extra special.

OR . . .

Glue on sequins and jewels or beads into an interesting design.

21 Hemming

Always tack first so you can ease in any fullness gradually.

22 Hooks and needles

Crochet hooks and knitting needles can be kept neat in plastic pages taped to secure the tops or with snap studs, in a folder.

23 Inserting zippers

This can be much easier to do when the fabric lies flat so insert before joining side seams.

24 Keeping buttons and lace

When you throw out an old garment, rescue buttons, lace and other trimmings for future use.

25 Keeping track of needlework.

Colour in the pattern lightly with pencil where you have already sewn; it will help identify where you are.

26 Keeping work clean

Wash your hands before sewing; any grease will mark your material or silks.

27 Knitting

Always finish the row before putting away.

28 Leftovers

Save small scraps and squares of cross-stitch fabric for making stitched decorations for gift tags and small greeting cards.

29 Maximum thread length

Ensure that your thread is no longer than the length from your fingers to just below your elbow. This will prevent knotting and fraying.

30 Minimum thread tip

Your thread should never be shorter than twice the length of your needle or your stitches will become too tight.

31 Needles

Leave a needle only in the margin of your tapestry or needlepoint, not in the main section where it can mark your work.

32 Needlework patterns

Place tulle or net over design, trace pattern, then position the fabric and trace design again. Remove fabric and join dots.

33 Needlework silks

To avoid colours running, silks should be washed before use and then dried flat.

34 Notebook covers

Cover notebooks and diaries with fur fabric, velour and crushed velvet. Glue into place with a glue gun and then decorate to taste.

35 Paintbrush holder

Store paintbrushes in florists' foam in a container.

36 Painting water

To keep water clear for longer, when changing paint colours, dip your brush into the water briefly, then wipe bristles on tissue or paper towel.

37 Paper patterns

Paper patterns rarely fit back neatly inside their original envelopes so store them in snap-lock plastic holders. If these are office hole-punched ones you can keep a neat file of all your patterns.

38 Pressing flowers

Pick fresh morning blooms. Let dew evaporate. Then dry in a flower press.

39 Quilting stitches

To ensure smooth stitching, first run the needle and thread through a piece of bees wax.

40 Revitalise potpourri

Sprinkle with essential oil and mix gently.
OR . . .
Add a few dried herbs.

41 Rubber stamps

Rubber stamps can be used to decorate boxes, candles, boxes, lampshades and hemlines.

42 Sew stationery

Use decorative sewing machine stitching on paper and envelope flaps to create your own personalised stationery.

43 Sewing machine care

Make sure your machine is serviced regularly.

44 Sewing machine needles

These should be replaced frequently before they are blunted.

45 Sewing machine pedal

Place this on a non-slip bathmat or rug so it stays put when sewing.

46 Sewing neat pleats

Use sticky tape to secure these in place, stitch through tape, and then remove.

47 Sewing-box

Fishing tackle or tool boxes make good reasonably-priced sewing boxes.

48 Sharper scissors

Keep fabric-cutting scissors very sharp. Cut into a sheet of sandpaper a few times to improve edges – or take them to a specialist.

49 Shoe boxes

Cover with paper and use to store cotton spools, letters, photographs, newspaper cuttings and so on.

50 Shoulder pads

Stitch old shoulder pads over coal-hangers to help clothes hang well and stay in shape.

51 Sleeve insertion

It is much easier to insert sleeves before joining side seams.

52 Stencil glue

Spray adhesive will hold stencils firmly in place but can be repositioned as needed.

53 Stencil sponges

Household or sea sponges are ideal for filling in tricky areas when painting.

54 Tapestry or needlepoint

Work the white areas of a design first. White threads worked later can be discoloured by surrounding threads.

55 Tension

If the tension on your sewing machine is erratic, check for lint, fluff or fabric between the tension discs.

56 Tissue paper craft

Save colored tissue paper, tear into small pieces and glue to gift boxes in a collage effect. Apply a decoupage glaze.

57 Travel kit

Plastic film canisters can hold emergency travel supplies of needles, buttons, safety pins and so on.

58 Trousers

Overlong trousers and jeans for a child can be turned up and held in place with a popper – easily removed when the youngster grows.

59 Zippers

These are expensive. Cut off and keep old ones when throwing out garments.

Money Matters

1   Acting as guarantor

Be wary of guaranteeing a loan. You may become liable to take over repayment.

2   Bank cards

Use a bank card to pay all your accounts and for shopping. It's easy – and cheap if you pay the card account in full each month.

3 Bank complaints

If you have can't get satisfaction over a complaint to your bank contact the ombudsman or equivalent who deal with disputes.

AND . . .

Always take time to double check bank statements for any errors.

4 Banking costs

Always check the cost of bank transactions each month. Check there are no unexpected changes or increases.

5   Banks

When choosing a new bank, look for special new client offers and compare all the options carefully.

6   Be responsible

Do read about how to make money work best, and take professional advice, but always research to ensure the choices will suit you, your family and your lifestyle.

7   Borrowing to buy

If you choose to borrow money to buy an investment, do ensure this will definitely increase in value. Choose a solid option.

8 Borrowing

Shop around. Negotiating can save money.

9 Budgeting

Plan your spending and home running costs. Keep track of invoices, payments and cash outgoings. Adjust budget as needed so it is realistic, you know where you are and can plan ahead.

10 Buy now, pay later

Companies often offer a special deal if you opt for paying in instalments but settle after say, 6 months or a year. Note this date clearly in your diary and pay before the deadline arrives or heavy instalment payments will become due.

11 Car choice

Be aware that apart from vintage vehicles, cars depreciate every year. Decide exactly how much you are prepared to lose.

12 Cash deals

If paying cash for large household items, always haggle for the best price, then ask if you can pay even less with cash. The answer is usually, yes.

13 Change

Be prepared to change banks, insurance, power suppliers and so on. Always make sure you have the best deal available.

14 Check spending

It is not what you earn, it is what you spend that will make a difference to future security. Save and invest as best you can.

15 Common-sense house purchase

Buy property in a pleasant area with job growth, recreational facilities, good schools and transport.

16 Credit card bonus

If you buy items with a credit card you may benefit from extra security and cover if there is a problem with the goods. Check the small print.

17 Credit card insurance

Always insure your credit cards against loss or theft.

18   Credit cards

Be aware that if you do not pay off credit cards at the end of the month, or obtain additional ones to make payments on the older ones, this can lead to ever-increasing debts.

19   Credit cards

Consider changing your credit card company regularly to maximise new client special deals and pay less interest.

20   Credit cards

If you use credit to pay for a vacation or large item do try to pay off the debt promptly before interest charges add greatly to the cost.

21 Enjoy income

While planning for the future, do make sure you gain pleasure from any extra money. Do not wait for ever to spend and enjoy it.

22 High return investments

Check carefully: high return will mean high risk.

23 Home buying

With rare, short-lived exceptions, houses increase in value each year and so buying a home is generally the best possible investment.

24 Investment scams

Double-check any deals that often offer vast returns for small outlay. They are rarely bona-fide.

25 Investment

If it looks too good to be true, it is!

26 Long term investment

Investing in well-located property and/or shares will grow your money best.

27 Low-interest car

Extend your mortgage to buy a car and pay low interest – but do change the mortgage repayments to pay off the debt as soon as possible.

28 Mortgages

A mortgage will add up over the years but the interest is generally far less than for a normal loan so adding to the mortgage is usually a cheaper option. Check it out.

29 Pensions

Start planning and saving as early as possible.

30 Personal loans

These can help sort out emergencies but be aware they can double the costs by the time they are repaid.

31 PIN numbers

Always guard your numbers carefully; do not leave any in your wallet. Memorise a new number on receipt and then destroy the notification.

32 Pocket money

Teach your children to save and to spend wisely.

33 Research

Do thorough research before investing. Ensure you understand all the implications and risks.

34 Retirement finances

Work out how much income you need: to retire at age 55, multiply income by 17; to retire at age 60, multiply income by 15; to retire at 65, multiply by 13.

35 Saving

Plan how much you want save. Then avoid the temptation to dip into it by putting this money where it cannot easily be tapped.

36 See an expert

Do not take financial advice from well-meaning friends or family without checking with the professionals too.

37 Sensible cover

Evaluate assets wisely. Do not over-insure – or under-insure.

38 Shares

A diversified portfolio will usually make money over the long term. Choose a variety of company types.

39 Tax and accounting advice

Sound advice can save good money and is a wise investment.

40 Tax deductions

Consult an accountant to ensure tax deductions are all as you suppose.

41 Tax returns

If the tax office owes you a tax refund, make sure your tax return form is sent in as early as you can. Then you can make use of these funds as soon as possible.

42 Tax-free investment

Paying extra on your mortgage can earn a high percentage – tax free and risk free.

43 Travel insurance

Never travel without proper cover. Medical costs, especially, can be prohibitive when abroad.

44 Wills

Make a will and update it regularly. If you want to keep costs down, find a special 'will-maker' rather than a lawyer, or buy 'do-it-yourself' forms.

Household Running
&
Appliances

1   Bank accounts – Check your bills

Mistakes do happen occasionally. Always study bank statements thoroughly and check each month against the previous one.

2   Building contract

Do organise a formal agreement and include starting and finishing dates, allowing for any delays due to bad weather or supply problems.

3   Building plan

Even if only minor tasks are involved (driveways, decks, roofing or fences) draw a diagram or plan, with measurements as part of the contract (useful if there is any dispute later).

4 Building progress

Allow for progress payments and include a withholding clause in case of defects.

5 Building work

Ask for at least 2 written quotes to cover all the work and materials to compare prices and approach.

6 Car checks

Never sign a contract, or pay a deposit until you have had a mechanical inspection by a licensed mechanic or motoring association.

7   Car deposits

A deposit does not necessarily give you the right to cancel without penalty. If you have signed an Offer to Purchase or equivalent, the dealer may be entitled to keep the deposit or a percentage of the car price if you cancel.

8   Car repairs

Should you have a disagreement with a car repairer, contact your local fair trading or consumer affairs office or equivalent. Motorists' associations can also help you sort out problems with their registered repairers.

9   Car services

Make sure you have a clear agreement with your garage or repairer to contact you first to authorise unexpected repairs or expenses.

10 Car viewing

Never inspect a car at night or in the rain when blemishes, dents and corrosion are less obvious.

11 Choosing a builder

Ask to see the builder's licence, and check its validity.

AND . . .

Try to see some work already done by the builder.

12 Defrosting the freezer

Do this as often as possible to avoid build up of ice and to keep it running efficiently.

13 Delivery dates

When choosing a new large appliance, always check delivery. The item in the showroom may not be in immediate stock and it is annoying to choose something only to discover that there is a long wait involved.

14 Entertainment items

As well as individual items, always check the price of combinations of televisions, videos, DVD's, sound systems and so on. A range of combined items may present excellent value for money.

15 Freezer and fridge capacity

To run efficiently, keep at least three-quarters full.

16 Freezers

If there is little food in there, fill spare space in the freezer with empty cardboard boxes so the freezer runs efficiently and costs are kept to a minimum.

17 Fridges & freezers

Never place in a very warm place or too close to your oven.

AND . . .

Ensure good air flow on all sides.

18 Home contents insurance

Make sure you update your insurance cover as you acquire new possessions.

19 Insurance and guarantees

Set up a filing system with all the paperwork in order. It is so much easier to find that essential document when something does go wrong.

20 Interest rates

Compare the rates and shop around for the best value.

21 Looking tidy

It can help the appearance of your kitchen or utility room if appliances are set behind matching doors but do show any visitors or baby-sitters where to find the fridge.

22 Mail order

This can be a slightly more expensive way to buy equipment but allows you to check the goods thoroughly first at home and to pay in a certain number of instalments without extra costs – so do your sums.

23 Mail-box offers

Beware of mail-shots for building work, pest control, carpet or upholstery cleaning and so on. Always check credentials and pricing.

24 New for old

In this throw-away society, repairs can prove very expensive. Do check the costs of replacement before paying very high repair bills.

25 New lines

Remember when a new line or style is introduced there may be excellent bargains to be had in the older models. Ask and see.

26 Power costs

Study the labels to check running costs of appliances.

27 Refund rights

'No refunds, no exchange' signs are illegal. You are still entitled to a refund or exchange if the product is faulty.

28 Reliable removers

Be prepared to pay a little more for a good, reliable service. Recommendation from a previous user of the company is to be welcomed.

29 Remote controls

Repairs or replacement of remote controls will be expensive. Keep in a safe place away from heat and direct sunlight, and especially from liquids or moisture and subsequent corrosion.

ALSO . . .

Excessive pressure on the buttons or casing can fracture the internal circuit board.

30 Removals

Obtain several written quotes which should cover removal cost, packing and carton cost if applicable, insurance and sometimes storage.

31 Sales

Remember that January and mid-year sales are an opportunity to buy household items at greatly reduced prices, as well as clothing.

32 Shopping by mail order

Never send money to a trader who uses a post office box number rather than a proper address.

33 Small removals and single items

Check if you can share space with another load.

34 TV screens

Apply a liquid fabric softener on a cloth to the screen surface. Do not let liquid run down screen and inside to circuitry.

35 Warranty cards

Always return the warranty card to the manufacturer. This provides a clear record of your purchase, and may provide extra benefits.

Children
&
Babies

1   Baby shampoo

Stand a baby shampoo bottle in the bath water for a few minutes to bring it up to temperature.

2   Bath/tub temperature

Check this with your elbow which is more sensitive to heat than your hands.

3   Baby-sitting

Join or form a baby-sitting circle with other local parents. As well as allowing you to take some evenings out, you will meet lots of new friends.

4   Bathtime

Wearing a cotton glove will help you to keep a firm hold on a very young, slithery baby.

5   Birthday balloons

Attach balloons with the children's names written on them to the back of the chairs as place names.

6   Birthday lollipops

Stick a bunch of lollipops into half a melon as a fun centerpiece on the party table.

7   Board game tip

Speed up the progress of Snakes and Ladders by using 2 dice.

8   Bunches of balloons

To decorate the room, blow up balloons and stick them to walls and ceilings with double-sided sticky tape.

9   Cake substitute

Turn a tub of vanilla ice-cream out onto a plate. Place chocolate buttons or small candies on the top to show the age. Decorate edge with chocolate fingers.

10 Candle holders

Use marshmallows as candle holders on birthday cakes. They look good and stop wax dribbling onto cake.

11 Chewing gum

To remove from clothing, pick off as much as possible, smother with olive oil and rub briskly with fingers.

OR . . .

Place garment in the freezer until the gum hardens and then pick off.

12 Covering books

When covering school books, wear an oven mitt to stroke out air out from adhesive paper.

13 Dice

Using 2 dice rather than one in a board game encourages children to add up and learn a few sums.

14 Dressing dolls

Some outfits are very tight-fitting. Sprinkle doll with talcum powder and the clothes will slip on and off more readily.

15 Early warning bell

Set a timer bell to remind youngsters when mealtime or bedtime is near. Allow them about 10 minutes to finish their game after the bell rings.

16 Fairy sandwiches

Use chocolate-hazelnut spread and then scatter hundreds and thousands.

17 Family far away

Make a collection of photographs of family or friends who live away for your children so they recognise them and know all these other folk when they do come to stay.

18 Family photos

Keep a photo album especially for your child. Include your immediate family, pets, trips and holidays shots.

19 Feeding unwilling mouths

Pretend the spoon is a plane, or train or boat, and make appropriate noises.
OR . . .
Use a glove puppet to deliver the meal.

20 Flannel fun

Children enjoy having their own matching coloured wash cloths and toothbrushes.

21 Flat pop

Freeze this to make ice lollies.

22 Hand puppet

Transform an old soft toy into a hand puppet, by cutting off the legs and removing the stuffing.

23 Holdall

A plastic bucket is an excellent way to take toys out when out visiting.

24 Holidays without parents

Pack sets of clothing in separate plastic shopping bags marked with the days of the week. This helps organise the child and keeps clean and dirty clothes separated.

25 Home-made puzzles

Paste a magazine picture onto cardboard and cut it into pieces appropriate to the child's age and competence.

26 Horrid sandwiches

Children will love the joke if the adult party host prepares some silly sandwiches filled with toy bricks, dominoes, plastic soldiers or crayons and then pretends to start to eat them.

27 Improvised night-light

Use a 25 watt blue bulb in the overhead light.

28 Insect bites

Take the sting out by rubbing with Marmite. The vitamin B content stops the itch and discourages further insect attack.

29 Jelly lollies

Use jelly instead of fruit juice to make delicious ice lollies.

30 Knitting

Boys and girls enjoy knitting. Start them off with 2 crochet hooks. They are easy to hold and the children will be less likely to drop stitches.

31 Labeling clothes

Use fabric paint to write on names. Once dry, it is permanent and does not fade.

32 Labels

Use bright nail polish to name lunch boxes and drink containers.

33 Letters for cards

Keep bored children amused by suggesting they cut out letters and pictures from magazines and save these in plastic folders. They can be used later to make birthday cards for friends and family.

34 Magazine letters

If children announce they are bored, suggest they cut out large colored letters from magazines and save these in plastic folders. Then, when schoolbooks need covering, the letters can be glued on to spell out their names and the subjects etc.

35 Mini-market

Trim labels from small-sized cans and packets and glue onto empty film canisters and boxes to make a toy shop.

36 Mug tree stand

Hang rattles and teething rings (or hair bows and hats) on a wooden mug tree for instant access.

37 Names on pencils

Order school pencils pre-named.

OR . . .

Shave off a strip of wood with a potato peeler and then write name.

38 Old Christmas cards

Children enjoy cutting out images from old Christmas cards, especially with pinking scissors. Punch a hole in these and add thread to make Christmas parcel tags.

39 Old clothes

Add new buttons or appliqués to make hand-me-down or old clothes more interesting.

40 Outgrown tracksuits

Tracksuits can be lengthened by adding bands of contrasting fabrics in arms and legs.
OR . . .
Cut off and turn into shorts.

41 Painting archive

Hang your children's school paintings together on a big bulldog clip behind the bedroom door.
OR . . .
Give them their own notice board for all such treasures.

42 Party bags

The birthday host will enjoy painting small brown paper bags for the parting gifts. They can be stuck down with brightly coloured paper clips or stars or stickers.

43 Party mayhem

If the noise level becomes unbearable, suggest a game of statues or 'Quiet Lions' or some such game that requires silence.

44 Party planning

Plan parties well, especially the games, to ensure a smooth flow and no time for rioting!
AND . . .
Organise a few committed helpers.

45 Photo collection

Order and keep spare pictures carefully so that you can give each child a set years later when they will be really appreciated.

46 Photograph puzzles

Many photographic developers will turn your snapshot into a tailor-made puzzle of your own child, house or pet.

47 Playgroup

If a rota involves parents, do remember that some grandparents too may be happy to take their turn.

48 Posters

Frame sections of giftwrapping paper for your child's bedroom.

49 Reviving a tired doll

Cream foundation and blusher can add colour to a faded face. Use nail polish on lips and waterproof mascara on eyelashes.

50 Sandpit cover

Plastic trellis will cover a sandpit, keeping animals at bay, but is light enough for children to remove themselves.

51 Sandwich pep up

Use humus dip instead of butter.

52 Sandwich shapes

Use a teddy bear or gingerbread-man biscuit cutter to cut sandwiches into fun shapes. Add currants or sultanas for eyes.

53 School label

To help very young children find the right bag, pop a photograph of them in the see-through label.

54 Sewing eyes

Dental floss is great for sewing limbs and eyes back onto soft toys.

55 Sharing food

Suggest one child cuts the 'share' – and the other chooses.

56 Sitting up

Pop a blow-up swim ring around the baby's waist to save all that initial toppling over.

57 Soup

Quickly cool a bowl of soup by breaking a slice of frozen bread into it.

58 Summer shade

Peg a sheet over the washing or rotary line to make a fun tent.

59 Table den

A sheet or blanket over the kitchen table makes a great den.

60 Teething gel

This will help numb the skin when you need to remove a splinter.

61 Toilet training

When toilet training a little boy, float a ping-pong ball in the bowl, with a bull's-eye painted on it to make aiming fun.

62 Toy book ends

Turn old soft toys into book ends by opening a seam, and filling with pebbles or sand.

63 Toy store

Hide away some toys that have been ignored for a while, and bring them out again when your child is bored or ill in bed.

64 Travel pack

A back-pack filled with toys, books and snacks can be slung from the front seat to provide entertainment on long journeys.

65 Walking home

Walking home from school instead of using the car gives you all extra exercise and creates a good opportunity to talk about the day's events.

66 Wearing them out

If it is a summer birthday party, outdoor races can use up lots of excited, excess energy.

67 Writing stories

Write out a simple tale, leaving gaps for the child to fill in, to encourage him or her to learn how to develop a story.

Computers
&
the Internet

1   Be organised

Use your computer to create lists of vital jobs, rosters, things to remember, essential 'everytime' groceries, and so on.

2   Busy times

Be warned that early evening and weekends are often hectic on the internet and it can be harder to make a connection.

3   CD cases

Keep CDs clean and safe in their cases. Buy spares from a stationery or computer store.

4   CD music

Keep a record of your music collection on your computer, for your own reference and for insurance purposes.

5   Computer cover

If light is interfering with your computer screen, invest in an anti-glare cover.

OR . . .

Buy a blind – or put something over the window while you are working.

6   Computer games

These are excellent for beginners to enjoy while they learn how to use the computer keyboard and mouse.

7   Computer shopping

Shopping via the internet is not only convenient but most sites allow you to create shopping lists that can be added to – so there is no need for any more scribbled notes.

8   Copy discs

Make duplications of precious items in case of any problems.

9 Crystal care

You can buy special crystals to place near the computer and so reduce the risk of exposure to electromagnetic rays and possible headaches.

10 Eye care

Do not work for protracted periods without taking your eyes off the screen.

11 Family occasions

Make a site with photographs of a wedding or new baby for other friends and family to visit.

12 Flash cards

These help a toddler learn to read. Make your own by printing large, bold words and sticking them to cards.

13 Good lighting

This is vital.

14 Hard copy

Always print out hard copy of precious documentation just in case of computer failure or theft.

15 Headaches

Avoid these by using an ioniser in the room to minimise the effects of electromagnetic rays.

16 Insurance

Make sure you have sufficient insurance cover for all your kit.

17 Internet dating

Be extremely cautious over supplying personal details, telephone numbers and addresses. If you do agree to meet, do so in daytime on neutral territory with an escape route pre-planned!

18 Internet discipline

Always make sure you disconnect properly from the internet. Turn off your modem when not in use.

19 Keep keys clean

Clean keyboard regularly and do not drop crumbs or debris between the keys.

20 Labels

Label discs and CDs clearly and file in order so you can always find which ones you want easily.

21 LED screens

These are believed to be safer to use long-term than are conventional screens.

22 Lighting

Use an adjustable desk lamp to direct light exactly where it is needed.

23 Liquids

Keep drinks well away from your computer.

24 Make separate folders

To keep files from family members or different jobs separate, create individual folders.

25 Mark your favorites

Tag the internet sites you visit regularly so it is easy to find them again.

26 Mouse

Avoid repetitive strain on the wrists by using wrist rests and not working too long on the same kind of activity.

27 Moving equipment

If in transit, keep your keyboard and mouse safe in an old stocking.

28 New programs

These are constantly updated but think before you buy: each new version means the user must learn new tricks. Moreover, the very latest one may still have teething problems.

29 Old friends

Various sites offer the means to contact old school friends and work colleagues. This can be very rewarding, compulsive – and very time consuming!

30 Photo sharing

If you have a scanner, create a digital photo collection to send to friends and relatives who have computers.

31 Plants

Keep pot plants, debris and water a safe distance from your computer.

32 Play safe

Save work regularly in case of a power failure or crash.

33 Posture

To avoid eye strain, your eye level should be level with the top half of the screen.

34 Pricing

Computers and programs are continuously becoming more efficient and less expensive so there are many excellent deals to be had now. Compare prices but bear in mind how much service and help each supplier is offering, too.

35 Stands and shelves

Buy stands for your screen and printer to elevate these and make more room underneath.

36 Storing CDs

If possible, keep duplicates of important CDs in separate places from the originals, so if there is flood, fire or theft, all is not lost.

Food
&
Drink

1   After the barbecue

Ensure barbecue is properly put out by pouring water or sand over it. Never put hot embers in a dustbin. Make sure gas bottles are turned off and no seals are leaking.

2   Alcohol

Alcohol is a useful ingredient and gives a distinctive flavour. If it is not available or allowed, use stock in savoury dishes and fruit juice in desserts.

3   Anchovies

Soak over-salty anchovies in milk for 20 minutes. Drain and rinse.

4   Avocados

To test if these are ripe, flick off the stalk. If it comes off easily, fruit is ripe.

OR . . .

Hold avocado in the palm of your hand and apply gentle pressure to stem end. If avocado does not yield at all, it is not yet ready.

5   Bacon and gammon

Slit edges before grilling and it will stay flat.

6   Baked apples

Stuff cooking apples with butter, honey and dried fruit and pour syrup over. Cover centre with foil to prevent fruit scorching.

7   Baked fruit

Keep fruit upright to ensure even cooking. Bake whole in a large container to retain fluid content.

8   Barbecue fuels

Never use petrol, paraffin, firelighters or oil. Once used, keep matches well clear.

9   Barbecue timing

Save time by pre-cooking some items like baked potatoes in oven or microwave and then finish them off on barbecue.

10 Barbecue safety

Keep a bucket of water or sand close by in case of emergencies.

11 Barbecue site

Choose a flat, level place, sheltered from wind, and ensure the barbecue stands steady.
AND . . .
Keep clear of fire risks, such as sheds, fences, and overhanging trees.

12 Bread maker

Ensure perfect bread making by investing in a new machine. They save a lot of hard work and create excellent results.

13 Browning meat

When cooking mince or cubes of meat, first sear in a hot pan until well browned.

14 Barbecue burns

Avoid wearing loose sleeves and use long-handled, well-insulated tools.

15 Buying a barbecue

Buy one with a lid that can be used to smother flames.

16 Cakes

To level top, return cooled cake to pan. Saw a serrated knife across surface, using edge of pan as a guide.

17 Cheesecake

This may shrink and crack, especially if overcooked. When baking time is complete, turn off oven, open door and leave cheesecake to cool slowly inside.

18 Chocolate

Run a vegetable peeler along a block of chocolate to make decorative swirls for cakes or desserts.

19 Citrus peel

Shred citrus peel and simmer in sugar syrup. Use for decorating cakes and desserts.

20 Cooking courgettes/zucchini

Brush lightly with oil and grill instead of frying.

21 Dressings

Mix salad dressing in a blender; it will not separate so quickly.

22 Dried herbs

One teaspoon of dried herbs equals one tablespoon of chopped fresh herbs.

23 Filo pastry

To stop this drying and cracking, cover with plastic wrap and a damp tea-towel.

24 Food lice

Kill these safely with a hot hair dryer.

25 Food safety

Cooking will normally kill harmful bacteria but do ensure meat is cooked all the way through by testing with a skewer until no pink juices run out.

26 Fresh barbecue food

Keep salads and dressings cold until required. Pack with ice if necessary.

27 Frozen meat

Do not take short cuts. Ensure that you always thaw meat fully.

28 Frying

Use stock rather than oil for tasty stir-frying.

29 Garden peas

To keep garden peas green, soak overnight in water with baking soda (sodium bicarbonate).

30 Gas barbecue purchase

Ensure this has a certified safety label and meets required standards.

31 Gas barbecue connectors

Make sure these are clean and tightly fitted in the correct place. Check connecting hose is well maintained.

32 Greens

Wash leaves, shake off excess water and cook very briefly in a covered pan without water, or in a microwave.

33 Herb vinegar

Put clean dry fresh herbs in a bottle. Fill with white wine vinegar and seal tightly. Keep refrigerated

34 Honey

To re-liquefy crystallised honey, stand jar, uncovered, in hot water, stirring until smooth.
OR . . .
Place uncovered jar in microwave on medium power for 20 seconds.

35 Keeping herbs fresh

Keep herbs fresh by placing stems in a jug with a little water; cover with a plastic bag and refrigerate.

36 Kiwi fruit

Slice off both ends and use a dessert spoon to push flesh from skin.

37 Light pastry

Make pastry in a cool place. Chill butter and water. Handle as little and as quickly as possible.

38 Lighting a barbecue

Get the barbecue going well before you plan to cook. It takes longer than you think to reach the right temperature.

39 Liqueurs

Keep lemon liqueurs in the freezer to achieve the right chill factor.

40 Meat

When frying, grilling or barbecuing meat, fish or poultry, turn only once or the flesh will dry out.

41 Nuts

Remove skins from hazelnuts by toasting in a moderate oven for 5 to 10 minutes. Wrap in a teatowel and rub well.

42 Oils

Warm on a low beat before brushing on food for grilling.

43 Onions

To reduce tears, freeze onions for 10 minutes or refrigerate for 1 hour before chopping.

44 Parmesan

Store in an airtight container in the freezer.

45 Parmesan

Use a vegetable peeler to slice off thin shavings for fruit or spaghetti.

46 Pastry and dough

Keep hands clean while working the mix by rubbing them with flour. After removing mix from bowl, soak this in cold water immediately.

47 Peppers or capsicums

Once cooked, cover with a damp tea-towel. They cool quickly and then the skins will slide away.

48 Perfect pastry

Leave pastry mix wrapped in plastic in the refrigerator for 30 minutes before and after rolling.

49 Pineapple

If crown leaf pulls off easily, the fruit is ready to eat.

50 Piping bag

Small, strong plastic bags are good for piping and for drizzling chocolate. Use and discard.

51 Prawns

Insert a fine skewer just behind the head, and then carefully draw out vein in one piece.

52 Raw and cooked food

Keep separate during storage and preparation. Use separate utensils for each.

53 Rice

Save leftover rice and freeze for later use.

54 Ripe bananas

Freeze, unpeeled, in an airtight container or bag. Thaw before mashing or use in banana cakes or muffins.

55 Safe barbecue food

Keep food covered, off the ground, and away from pets.

56 Short crust pastry

If food processing, use short, quick bursts of power. Use only just enough water to blend ingredients.

57 Skewers

To stop bamboo skewers splintering or scorching, soak in water for one hour before use.

58 Skimming fat

Make soups and stocks. Refrigerate for a day and then remove fat 'skin'.

59 Skinning fish or chicken

Dip your fingers in salt to provide a good grip.

60 Syrup and honey

Stop honey or syrups sticking to your spoon by running it under hot water first.

61 Thin sliced meat

Cover raw meat in plastic wrap and partially freeze. Then unwrap and slice.

62 Tomatoes

Store in egg boxes. Do not chill.
AND . . .
Peel them more easily in a jug of hot water.

63 Turn plain flour into self-raising

Add 2 teaspoons of baking powder to each cup of plain flour.

OR . . .

Add 1 teaspoon of cream of tartar and ½ a teaspoon of bicarbonate of soda to one cup of plain flour.

64 Yoghurt

Use instead of sour cream in savoury recipes. Cool pan for a few minutes before stirring in.

Travel Tips

1 Avoid pickpockets

Be wary of strangers who offer to help. They may be looking for an easy target.

2 Books

Always take a couple of good books to read on the plane, bus or train, or for times when the weather keeps you indoors.

3 Cameras

To deter snatch-and-grab thieves, disguise expensive camera gear in an old carry bag or haversack.

4 Car mirrors

Wipe down with a damp cloth and washing up liquid and let dry naturally. The mirror will stay clear for much longer.

5 Car windscreens/windshields

Wipe inside with a damp cloth and washing up liquid and let dry naturally.

6 Carry a pen

Be sure to carry a pen in your bag. Sometimes you have to fill in forms in the most unusual places.

7   Check-in times

For international flights, check-in is usually two hours before the scheduled departure, and for domestic services, at least half an hour before the flight. Check your tickets and information.

8   Children

If taking youngsters with you, find out if there are child-minding facilities or a children's club where you are staying. Make sure you are not miles from the beach or centre of activities.

9 Claiming on insurance

If you lose luggage or other valuables, report it to the airline, hotel and police immediately. Your insurer will need verification of loss or theft – and proof that you have taken steps to recover the item.

10 Clothes

Most people take too many clothes on holiday, so be sensible about what you really need. Choose items that mix and match for variety.

11 Crease-proof clothes

Choose clothes that need little or no ironing. Rolling up rather than lying flat will fill awkward corners in the case.

12 Credit cards

Check that your card can be used overseas. This can be useful for unexpected purchases and if you run short of funds.

13 Dental care

Visit the dentist for a check-up before you leave. Toothache can ruin a holiday.

14 Directions

When in a country with a high crime rate, don't stand in the street consulting a map. Ask for directions in a store, hotel or police station, or go indoors to study your tourist guide.

15 Diving

Ensure your instructors are experts with a recognised PADI or BSAC qualification.

16 Documents

Make a copy of traveller's cheque numbers.
Photocopy your passport and travel documents
and carry these copies in a different part of your
luggage from your travel documents. These
copies could be invaluable if the originals are
lost or stolen.
Leave a copy at home with relatives, too.

17 Don't accept low standards

Should your accommodation not measure up,
complain immediately and ask to be moved to a
better room. If traveling in a group, complain to
the tour leader. If all else fails, negotiate a
reduction in the charge.

18 Don't sit down

In Europe, drink your coffee standing at the bar – it will be much cheaper than having it at a table and, as a bonus, you will have a chance to talk to the locals.

19 Driving license

Take this with you if you are thinking of hiring a car when abroad.

20 Emergency repairs

Empty plastic film canisters can hold emergency travel supplies of needles, buttons, safety pins and so on.

21 First-aid kits

Never leave home without a simple first-aid kit – painkillers, indigestion tablets, anti-diarrhoea pills, sunburn cream, bandages, elasticised patches for blisters and sun protection.

22 Flying and diving

Never dive within 24 hours of flying.

23 Going topless

Check out the local response. It may be the norm on some beaches but in certain countries will offend locals. You may even be arrested.

24 Hair dryers

Take a small hairdryer and dual fittings or plugs.

25 Hand luggage

Ensure your hand luggage is an acceptable size
to prevent problems at the airport.

26 Handbags and wallets

Always tidy your handbag or wallet before going
away and remove any unnecessary clutter.

27 Health checks

Ensure you are fully aware of any health risks. Your travel agent and doctor can advise, or consult a medical or vaccination centre at least 6 weeks before you travel. Some countries require proof of vaccination.

28 Hidden extras

Beware of extra costs, particularly on cruises. Drinks and shore excursions are rarely included.

29 Holiday list for helpers

Keep a permanent list on the fridge or notice board of jobs to be done in your absence. Then, when you go away, any friend helping can clearly see what is needed – how much cat food to give, which plants need watering, mobile telephone numbers and so on. This saves precious time when rushing off.

30 Holiday list: advance jobs

Keep a permanent list of *advance* jobs to be done.

Give contact numbers to neighbour, phone kennels, clean shoes, sort wash bags, order currency and travellers' cheques etc.

Then you do not have to rethink every time you go away.

31   Holiday list: last-minute 'red-tape' checks

Keep a permanent list to check the following are handy – passports, tickets, health insurance, foreign currency and travellers' cheques, hotel addresses.

32   Holiday list: last-minute 'grabs'

Keep a permanent list of *last-minute* things to remember to collect (alarm clock, pills, toothbrush etc.)

33 Holiday list: last-minute jobs

Keep a permanent list handy of *last-minute* jobs to be done (turn off immersion heater, give keys to neighbour, water indoor plants, etc.)

34 Holiday list: packing

Keep a permanent list of *advance* things to pack, over and above clothes (snorkels, mosquito repellent, sun tan oil and after-sun, books to read, etc.)

35 Holiday postcard list

Keep a permanent list to take away with you of postcard recipients.

36 Immersion heater/water heater

Turn this off when you leave but organise a friend to switch it on again the day before you return.

37 In-flight comfort

In the dry, air-conditioned atmosphere, skin dries out, so keep applying moisturiser.

38 Insurance

Ensure your cover is realistic. It is easy to underestimate the value of what you might lose.

39 Insurance

Never travel without insurance if you're going overseas. Health care costs – particularly a hospital stay – can be prohibitive.

40 Insurance

Read the small print on your travel insurance policy carefully. You may not be covered for injury in certain sports or activities.

41 Irons

Always take a travel iron for a quick freshen-up of clothes.

42 Just in case . . .

Always carry the address and phone number of the nearest diplomatic post or embassy, in case of an emergency.

43 Keep drinking

Jet lag and long flights dehydrate the body so avoid alcohol and eat light meals. When you arrive, take things gently for the first day.

44 Languages

Do learn some basic phrases and carry a phrase book with you at all times.

45 Leave an itinerary

In case of an emergency, leave an itinerary and contact numbers with relatives.

46 License

Make sure you consult a licensed travel agent who pays into a Travel Compensation Fund in order to compensate consumers and/or get them home again if the travel company fails.

47 Luggage straps

These will prevent spillage if the suitcase catch should fail and makes it harder for thieves to 'break in' quickly. Some airports offer a wrapping service to protect your luggage from any outside interference.

48 Luggage identification

Use obvious bright labels or colourful straps or straps with your name on to make your case distinctive on the airport carousel.

49 Magazines

Treat yourself to a magazine or collection of puzzles and crosswords to do in the airport, on the plane and while relaxing on the sun lounger.

50 Medical checks

If you have a medical condition, do check with your doctor that it is safe to travel and to fly.

51 Medication

Take a letter with you from your doctor, explaining what your tablets are and why you need to take them. It could save problems at customs and will be useful if you need to replace them for any reason.

52 Mixing cases

Don't pack 'his and her' cases. Always mix clothes so if one case vanishes in transit you can cope for a few days.

53 Mobile phone

Call your service provider to arrange a service abroad if you need this. It is not automatic. And collecting any messages needs a special code when you are overseas.

54 Motor insurance

Ensure this is all up to date – and it is a good idea to organise extra cover if driving distances.

55 Motoring abroad

If you plan to hire a car overseas, check whether you need an international driver's licence. Your local motoring organisation will be able to help.

56 Notebook

Always keep a tiny notebook to hand to write down lists of things to remember, buy, or do!

57 Packing

Always pack absolutely essential items like medicines plus a few pieces of underwear and a bathing costume in your hand luggage in case your main luggage ends up at the wrong airport.

58 Passport photos

Do take several spare passport-size photographs for entry visas, train passes and so on.

59 Passport

Check you can locate your passport in good time. Then check the expiry date. Has it expired or is it about to expire? Six months left to run is often required.

60 Passports

On the journey, keep these handy in a special pocket or handbag section, not buried under clutter.

61 Pets

Organise and inspect the kennels or cattery before leaving your pet.

62 Phone home

If you cannot use a mobile phone abroad, organise a phone credit card, which can be used to make calls from overseas, charged to your home number.

63 Plugs

Always pack a travel sink plug or a squash ball which makes good emergency plug for the bath.

64 Postcard addresses

Typed up sticky labels with friends' names and addresses greatly speeds up the postcard operation while you are away.

65 Power plug

Take plugs or travel adapters suitable for the country to which you are travelling. You can get these at a luggage or department store or at the airport shop.

66 Pregnancy

Check with the airline if you are allowed to travel at the stage of pregnancy concerned.

67 Road tolls

If driving on toll motorways, fix a little pouch or container at the front of the car for holding tickets and ready cash.

68 Receiving mobile phone calls

Be aware that generally phone calls received abroad on your mobile will be charged to YOUR account not to the caller.

69 Respecting cultures

When travelling away, especially into Islamic countries or when entering places of worship, check what is acceptable clothing. Shorts may be frowned upon, shoes may have to be taken off and women may need a scarf handy to cover their heads.

70 Safe cash and valuables

If the hotel offers safe boxes, do use these.

71 Secure your home

Leave a light on and the radio playing.

Cancel paper deliveries.

Organise a neighbour to collect the mail each day.

Leave a phone number where you can be contacted in an emergency.

72 Spectacles

Take a spare pair with you in case of loss or breakage. Take your prescription too. Some countries can make spectacles at a far more rational price than at home.

73 Stay awake

It is easy to doze on a train or bus. Ensure your valuables are kept out of sight and tie your bag to the seat.

74 Swollen ankles

Feet and ankles can swell in hot weather and on a long flight, so wear comfortable stretchy shoes and slip them off if necessary.

75 Thrombosis risk

Exercise as best you can on flights, especially long ones. Keep the feet moving and wear support socks if possible.

76 Tips

Check with your travel agent, hotel staff, or courier on what is 'the norm'.

77 Traveller's cheques

These are the safest way to carry money abroad. Check first which currency cheques to obtain for where you are going.

78 Travel sickness

Keep travel sickness tablets at hand. Ginger is an effective alternative.

79 Trolleys

Invest in a fold-out travel trolley if you have a heavy case, or buy a case with wheels.

80 Upset tummy

Always drink boiled or bottled water.
Avoid raw vegetables, salads and shellfish.
Peel fruit.
Avoid ice cubes: they can carry bacteria.

81 Valuables

It is safer to take jewellery and other valuables
with you onto an aircraft.

82 Weather

Check with the local tourist authority for things
to do in the event of wet weather.

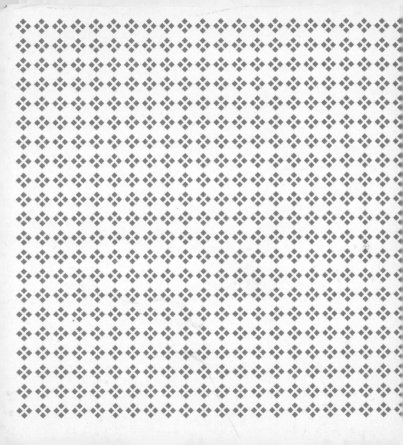